Goddess

Goddess

Visit www.booksurge.com to order additional copies.

Goddess

Memoir Of A Transsexual

Raquel Reyes

2007

ACKNOWLEDGMENTS

There are many people I feel indebted to for several reasons. Most certainly there were an important few who were instrumental in the creative process of this book. My friend Ricardo Farne was the one who above all encouraged me to tell my story and styled me for the beautiful cover photo. Joseph and Geeta Moore of Pip Printing in Tampa who assisted with the many tasks it took to submit my manuscript for publication. My photographer, Billy The Kid, who took the amazing cover photo as well as many others throughout my career. My friend Travis Sawyer for his wonderful input and expert graphic design.

A special shout out to the "superstars" of Tampa, both gay and straight, living and gone, all of whom supported, inspired, accepted and loved me throughout the years but because of space limitation could not be mentioned in my story. They include but are not limited to: Rico, Corey, Jen and Bill, Mike D, Shelby and Gary, Liz and AJ, Danielle, Ally and Stan, Raphael, Christine, Lisa, Robin, Meka, Beth and Andy, Krissy, Rick, Chris Howard, Ralph, Alfredo, Anthony G, Christian Bradshaw, Eddie, Carlo, Cord, Freddy, Guy and Lexi, Pauley, Travis, Mindy, Leslie, Orlando, Brian P, Brian Q, Joe, Ruben and Steve, Kirk Bocker (and the rest of the Bocker clan) , Zaul, Felix, Big Felix, Peachy and Ron, Michelle and Andrew, Temple, Jolene, Angel, Arlene, Darlene, Brenda, Charlie, Lakesha Lucky (Bianca), Candi Stratton, Kelly Anderson, Apple Love, Shauna Brooks, Tiffany Middlesexx, Michelle Maulden, John and Lori Benson, Mike and Joanne, and anyone else I may have forgotten or was unable to mention. You guys have always meant the world to me.

The owners and various staffs of Thee Dollhouse, 2001 Odyssey, Shangri-La, Mons Venus, Hyde Park Café, Bahasa Lounge, Jackson's, The Palm, and countless other places in Tampa, Boston and Miami that know and respect me and put up with my sometimes irritating habit of bringing an entourage and still comp me drinks and cover.

The editors of V2 who took a chance by putting me on the cover of their magazine not once but twice and never regretted their decision.

Bubba The Love Sponge for his support and for bringing me to the attention of a whole new audience.

A very special thank you to R.K. for the many good times we shared and the love and friendship you continue to offer. You are truly a great man and mean the world to me...now and always.

Hiran, who should have had a bigger part in the book but settled for a bigger part in my life...and in my heart.

And of course, Gregory, who came to mean so much to me. My friend and confidant and the one who truly makes Savannah feel like home- for so many beautiful reasons. Thank you for being a very special part of my life and of my heart. Always.

Several important people in my life including certain family members and friends have been left out of this story at their request. In addition, certain names and situations have been changed or slightly altered to protect the innocent and the guilty.

For Charlie- who lived too fast and died too young.

"I've been things and seen places"
Mae West

PREFACE

I never thought of myself as a drug addict. I never considered myself a prostitute. When you earn $3000.00 a day, sleep with rock stars, porn stars and millionaires, fly first class to glamorous destinations throughout the world and mix with the so-called beautiful people, I think it's safe to say that your reality can become a bit distorted. When you're a transsexual who lives as a woman and lives better than most of the beautiful women you know, reality as you know it no longer exists. This is my story and it's unlike any story you've ever read. It has been a journey of self discovery that has left me with more questions than answers. But it is my life, for better or worse. And through it all, I learned much, lost more and came to accept only one complete truth. Though I often sold my body, perhaps even a part of my soul and the illusion of love to many, I gave my heart- my very real heart- to only two. That is the one thing I know for sure. The one true thing. But I won't jump the gun. Let me share with you the story of my incredible, high-heeled life.

CHAPTER I

I was a happy healthy baby boy when I entered the world on November 30th of some random year that always slips my mind. My mother told me years later that the most difficult thing about my birth was hearing my drunken father being removed from the room by hospital security. Other than that, it was a pretty painless procedure. She spit me out in about 45 minutes. I couldn't wait to get out. Isn't it funny how you just cant wait to get out...then you spend the rest of your life searching for the kind of safety and security you only find In the womb. My early years were easy. My mother, Emelia and my sister Josette were not just my immediate family. They were my family. They were everything I had aside from a loving aunt that would baby sit and a father that went to prison when I was 6 months old. Cousins and assorted family members would pop in and out of our lives when they were feeling generous with their time but for the most part it was just the three of us and it remained that way for most of my childhood. You see, Mama was the black sheep of the family. She married young and her choice in men was never the best so the family had just kind of turned their backs on her. Husband number one and the father of my sister was a renowned drug dealer and drug addict who kept Mama in diamonds and furs until he lost it all including his freedom. Husband number two was my good looking rogue of a father...A notorious New Orleans bad boy with a soft spot for the good life who made money any way he could accept honestly. Both men loved her madly and would continue to provide for the three of us to the best of their ability from where they were which wasn't easy. But as far as the family was concerned- well, that go-go boot, wig wearing party girl could just take those two little kids and her crazy husbands and find her own way...And that's just what Mama did. She found her own way. She became the very thing

I would become years later. A survivor. She did what she had to do to provide for her children. For better or worse, that is what I remember most about Mama.

My mother was quite a woman. Funny how you never really see the big picture until your much older or they're long gone. She worked long and hard to provide for me and my sister and she never took the easy road- a quality that I much admired in her. Growing up in Tampa, FL in the early seventies wasn't a picnic. There weren't very many job opportunities for a single mother raising two children. Often times, Mama went hungry to feed us and I remember all too well how she would cry when she thought we were asleep. Still, she did everything she could to keep us happy. We always had the best of everything. Clothes, toys…we even went to private school though I have no idea where the money came from. With the little money she made working at St. Joseph's Hospital, she was struggling just to keep a roof over our heads. But without fail, every Friday, Mama would rent a car, buy me and my sister a new outfit and drive all the way to Ocala to see my father. As a child, I thought it normal to visit your father behind bars and barbed wire. But I learned later that nothing about my life was normal. It never would be. My father, by all accounts, was a career criminal. Mostly racketeering and trafficking although the heist that put him behind bars for what became the next 27 years was a score worth over $800,000.00 dollars most of which was never recovered. He was very loving though and he adored his family in the purest sense. I have a lot of my father in me. I inherited his stunning good looks and his love of easy money. One always facilitates the other you know…

***

Fast forward to 1981. My mother had been standing by her man for quite a long time when it became painfully clear that my dad wasn't getting out anytime soon and Tammy Wynette just didn't know what the fuck she was talking about. By this time, my mom had been seeing quite a bit of a man named Johnny. Even though this book is about a Diva, not a Dickhead, we have to pause collectively , take a deep breath and get to know a little bit more…about Johnny. His friends called him Pulo which I always thought was a ridiculous name. I called him that at first…later I called him daddy. Eventually, I called him every name in the book- to his face and behind his back. But that comes later. He was an old-fashioned kind of guy. He was a kid raised on the streets and manhood had not done much to curb his street sensibilities or his machismo. But looking back, that must have been what initially attracted Mom to him. She loved her bad boy's, a trait I came to inherit. Speaking from experience, I know there is nothing like a really good…bad boy. They are so hot and passionate and rough. They are also abusive, destructive and prone to fits of rage and melancholy. Oh what a mix! That coupled with his relatively good looks and ready supply of cash made him the lucky winner of Mom's manhunt. You see, what I didn't know then was that the most important thing to mom at that moment was providing for her children. She could have left my sister with her grandparents or given me up to my aunt…but she didn't choose the easy way out. She decided that her children were the most important thing in her life and if she had to sacrifice her own happiness to provide for us a better life, then so be it. If she could have seen what lay ahead, I wonder if she might have changed her mind.

Around the time that Mom moved Johnny in and he became the king of all he surveyed, I noticed a change in myself and in the way other children were treating me. I had always been able to get along with just about everyone although I was a bit of a mama's boy. But now, children avoided me. They laughed at me and I didn't know why. Adults always commented on what a beautiful child I was. I remember the word beautiful. They never used the word handsome or cute. My clothes were always the best that money could buy even before we could afford it. I didn't know what I was doing wrong. Everyone loved my sister, especially the little boys. Why didn't they like me? The answer became painfully evident one day when I tried to play with some kids in the courtyard of the apartments where we lived. "We don't play with sissies. You look like a girl and you act like one too," they screamed. They laughed and left me standing there wondering what they meant. This would by no means be the first time I would encounter this kind of prejudice and cruelty from other children. But that very instant became a defining moment in my life. A moment that would stay with me forever. A moment that would repeat itself time and time again throughout my young life.

CHAPTER 2

I've never been big on rehashing my tragedies. Suffice to say, I hard a hard life. Big deal! I like to think I turned out okay in spite of everything. So instead of dedicating pages and pages of text to the ass-holes that made my life miserable between the ages of 9 and 18, I am going to give you the dime store version of my hellacious adolescence. Stepfather was an asshole. The 24 karat kind. The violent, abusive kind. Mother became an alcoholic to deal with it. Children suffered the consequences. The fighting that went on at home was legend in our neighborhood. School for me was no picnic either. Kids made fun of me- openly calling me a fag and generally doing anything to embarrass me. I had no refuge and very few friends. What I did have was my writing, my love of literature and my fascination with classic film stars. Those were the three things that brought me some degree of happiness during those years. I often wondered what it would be like had I been born into another family…a normal family. Things seemed so upside down in my world that it took every bit of cour-age just to go on. I often thought about death. I prayed to God but wasn't sure if he was listening. I went on praying nonetheless. I had so many questions. Why was I different? Why did I like boys instead of girls? Why did I want to be a girl? Why did I get stuck with an abu-sive stepfather…and what happened to my mother? The fun loving, beautiful woman I remembered was no more. She worked till 6 in the evening and started drinking at 6:30 so I had a good 45 minutes of sober time if I was lucky…and this went on for years. I escaped fur-ther into my dreams and writings and into my movies. I saw Scarface for the first time and became obsessed with Michelle Pheiffer. Her character, Elvira, represented everything I thought a woman should be. Beautiful, glamorous, sexy. Unfortunately, she was also an addict in the film and I thought that was glamorous too. No one told me different. This became another defining moment in my life. When left to my own devices and to draw my own conclusions, the outcome was never the best.

As the years dragged on and the children became teenagers and life became even more unbearable at school, I held to the belief that something better was waiting for me. Something big! It had to be. This couldn't be all there was. I wanted so many things. I wanted to travel, sip champagne, drop thousands on clothes, make love with handsome, wealthy men and try cocaine with beautiful people in exotic situations. Sure, I had a few friends at school but no one I could really share my hopes and dreams with…and even if I did, would they understand? I desperately needed someone to connect with. Someone I could confide in that wouldn't laugh at me. Someone…older. Ironically, I found my confidant in a very unusual place. A family barbeque reintroduced me to a distant cousin who hadn't seen me in years. A onetime party girl, full-time open-minded gift from God named Celeste. We chatted that day and I connected with her in a way that I had never connected with anyone.

There was an honesty there- a truth that so many people in my family were lacking. She seemed to pick up on the fact that I might need a friend because she offered her phone number and told me to give her a call sometime.

"I have a little girl and I don't really go out as much as I used to," she said.

"Okay, we can just get together and watch movies or something," I replied.

"That sounds great, Call me this weekend."

From that moment on, Celeste became a very important part of my life. I confided in her about my mothers drinking, how my step father caused havoc and chaos and how the kids at school were unbearably mean to me.

"Things can be rough when you're young," she said trying to comfort me, "but when you get a little older you'll realize that it's your life and it's what you want to make of it that determines real happiness. This part is just a short stop on the tour. It's never going to be easy but at least one day it will be yours. Your life, your choices, remember that."

"But what is happiness?" I asked.

"That's for you to decide. What do you want out of life? What are your dreams? What is it that you want more than anything and fuck what other people think. You know you can tell me anything..."

I couldn't believe what I was hearing. For the first time in my life, someone was asking me what I wanted. Talking to me as an equal and asking me to throw caution to the wind- to pursue my vision of happiness. I had no choice but to unburden myself. I cried and told her everything. I told her I thought I was gay, that I had to break away from my family and live the life I wanted. That I wanted to have the world and everything in it but didn't know how to go about getting it. That I thought I would have been better, more attractive, more popular had I been born a girl. She listened, really listened. Then she looked at me in that all-knowing way of hers and said the only thing she could say.....

"That's a lot and I understand...but what would make you happy right now?"

"I want to go to a gay bar," I replied

Celeste took a long look at me. We had been hanging out for awhile now. She knew this was no whim. She knew it was for real... and she knew it was something I needed to do.

"Then let's go to a gay bar," she said.

I was 16 years old.

CHAPTER 3

Celeste called her friend Mark- and he was the typical run of the mill homosexual you see everyday with a crossed eye thrown in for good measure- and off we went to a club called Paradise. First thing I see stepping out of the car? The most gorgeous man I think I had ever seen (at that time) carrying the bags of an equally beautiful woman that looked more like a Vegas showgirl than a connoisseur of dirty gay bars. The guy at the door knew Mark, gave me the once over and didn't ask to see my id which was just as well because I didn't have one. I stepped inside and felt a rush like nothing I had ever known. The rush was like a drug rush- like the first line of coke or the first time you drop X- it was nothing short of spectacular. The place was filled with men and I loved it. I was young and cute and yes, they all wanted my skinny little ass that night though Celeste did a great job of keeping the sharks at bay. The Vegas showgirl appeared again flanked by her hunky hanger on. She kissed Mark and Celeste, smiled at me and walked away. She was beautiful. She looked like Jerry Hall only better. Long, cascading blonde hair, a beautiful face and body...And she was a man. I was stunned. I tried to follow her to the bathroom but she slammed the door in my face after politely telling me that fans were not allowed in the dressing room. Fan? Who the hell was this person and what on earth had given her the idea that I even knew who she was let alone worshipped her? I didn't even know who she thought she was. But in that one moment, I learned a lot about queens. Some are great, some are not so great. Some are beautiful, some are beasts...and every last one of them can be a solid gold bitch...even the nice ones.

Needless to say, I was hooked on Paradise. I went back the next weekend to see the show and learned the queen's name was Crystal Clear. She was much nicer the second time around. She actually hit on me and it was quite flattering in a sloppy, drunken kind of way. But she was beautiful and Crystal I would learn years later as I developed into a girl was beautiful inside too. And at that time, in that place, she was every inch a star. I tried to be attracted to her but I couldn't. I didn't want her. I wanted to be her. She seemed to understand because she gave up on me and walked away. A few minutes later, the bartender came over and asked to see my id. Of course, I didn't have one and he asked me to not come back until I was 21. I could tell by the look on his face that he knew that wouldn't be for quite awhile. I left Paradise that night and didn't step foot in that bar again for several years. I also didn't see Crystal again for quite awhile. But that was alright. I was about to meet two people that would change my life forever. One was named Ruben and the other was named Esme Russell.

CHAPTER 4

Sometimes you meet a person and they immediately feel like family. Such was the case with my childhood friend Ruben. He was a petite flower also, if you know what I mean. He was a few years older than me and had recently "come out" to his family. I really wanted a friend that could relate to me. Celeste was great but she was a mother and she was a great mother. She couldn't go out that much. Ruben gave me his number and said to call him. I told him I was only seventeen. He said that didn't matter. He knew a place where they loved young guys and it wouldn't be a problem. We made plans to meet that Friday. He picked me up at my parent's house and we hightailed it with a lesbian friend of his to a place called The Carousel Club. As clubs go, it really didn't get much worse than this. A gay male strip club where gay for pay male porn stars got naked on stage and simulated sex. I loved it. And amidst all this madness, I saw her. The most beautiful woman I had ever seen. Her name was Esme Russell and this is where the story really gets good.

The Carousel Club was really jumping that night. It was packed to capacity because the legendary Joey Stefano was appearing on stage. Joey was, at the time, the most famous gay porn star in the world. The lights and club music dimmed signaling the beginning of the show. The show music kicked in—*Diana Ross's I Want Muscles*. I will never forget that song or that moment.

The fog cleared and onto the stage she stepped. She was absolutely breathtaking. I had never seen anyone like her. Crystal, by comparison, seemed like Pa Kettle. She was tall and exotic with a beautiful head of hair, high cheekbones and incredible lips. But when she dropped the zebra coat she was wearing, my mouth really fell open. A body that can only be described as Playboy perfection. She was in a corset, thigh highs and garters and as she stalked the stage like a hungry panther, I melted. She was IT. Her body was nothing short of awe-inspiring. Perfect DD breasts, a flat stomach, curves that literally went on forever. While every homo in the place screamed for the muscle boys surrounding her, I screamed for her and only her. I had found the one I had been searching for my whole life. You would have thought God himself had appeared before me. I was completely, utterly out of my mind. She saw me, standing in front, struggling to get a closer look at her. She was coming to the end of the song now and I saw that people were offering her tips on stage. I pulled $5.00 out of my jeans and held it out to her. She smiled as she took the money, kissed my cheek and turned to exit the stage. I looked over at Ruben and he could see the look on my face.

"Who is that?" I asked.

"That was Esme Russell," he replied.

"She's stunning."

"Yes, she is. She is also a bitch so steer clear…that queen is not a very nice person. That is putting it mildly."

"I have to meet her."

Ruben glanced over at me with a puzzled look in his eye. "Why?"

"I just do. I want to know her. And I don't care how rude she may be to me, but I'm going to introduce myself."

Of course, she was rude and arrogant and all the things Ruben said she would be. In fact, she was worse. I can say this now because today Esme is a very different person than she was and is still very close to my heart. But at the time, no one would have accused her of being Miss Congeniality. For some odd reason, perhaps out of a deep, burning, necessity for…a ride, she chose to accompany me and Ruben that night to an after hours spot called The Bridge Club. I was in love with her immediately. Esme had some unusual habits. She didn't speak to you as much as speak at you. She was very loud and dramatic. She was bitchy and self absorbed. If she wasn't talking about herself, she wanted to know what you thought of her. Ruben found it strange and frightening. I found it fascinating. We arrived at The Bridge Club and it was definitely the late night place to see and be seen if the strange cast of characters were any indication. It must have been what Studio 54 was like if Studio 54 had been a run-down barn made of tin with a dirt dance floor and a couple dozen drag queens and drug addicts running about. I must have looked like a small town girl in the big city because my mouth just dropped open. I was like Alice in Wonderland- everything, absolutely everything, was fascinating to me. Esme really made an entrance and everyone seemed to flock around her. I felt quite proud to be with her until I realized she was completely ignoring me. Ruben rolled his eyes, very bored with her antics. His look said "I don't have to know her, to know her." I realized at that moment that it was 5:00 am and I had to get home. That would probably be the last time that 5:00 am realization would ever hit me. I tracked Esme down, managed to get her number and left with Ruben. As I headed home I reflected on the night and how great it had been. I didn't know it then but I was at the very beginning of a new way of life. One that would involve glamour, excitement, new friends...and drugs!

CHAPTER 5

Ruben and I saw a lot of each other over the next few months. He continued to sneak me into several of the gay hotspots on both sides of the bay- Howard Avenue Station, 2606, Bedrox, etc. As our friendship developed, we became more open about our feelings and our hopes and dreams. Ruben wanted to be a woman, meet a great guy and raise a family. I was shocked. I couldn't believe what I was hearing. Finally, someone who felt the way I did. I don't know why but I decided to keep my feelings and gender-bending aspirations to myself. Believe it or not, I was ashamed. Esme too had become somewhat of an ally though she was constantly pushing me to come out to my family.

"You will never be happy until you accept yourself for what you are and who you are," she would say. "Your family is just going to have to understand."

Home life was becoming unbearable. I was having to come up with new and inventive stories to explain my constant disappearing act. I rarely saw my family, if ever. My mothers drinking had by now reached mythical proportions and I just decided that it was easier to stay away then watch her destroy herself. I fell deeper into my seductive new lifestyle and my strange and exciting new friends became a kind of surrogate family. With them, I could do anything. I felt I belonged. I felt powerful, I felt loved! And the family was growing. As my partying got the best of me and I slipped further into the vortex of endless nights and mornings that seemed to go as quickly as they came, a new crop of gay superheroes had emerged on the scene. Ricky- the beautiful, hopelessly optimistic dancer. Francisco- the razor-tongued dress designer who came to believe in me as strongly as anyone ever would. Hector- Ricky's lady in waiting who was still young enough to know he had a lot to learn but when he did...Oh boy, did he! Hiran- the kind, charismatic young man who became my dearest friend and remains one of my dearest to this day. There were others too, but these were the key players in my cast of illusions. They were there in the beginning. They are the ones who can truly say *I knew her when*. Yes indeed, these are the ones who helped create a monster.

CHAPTER 6

"Miss Thing, you are way too feminine to be a boy. Have you ever done drag?" The voice that called out to me that night was high and melodious and full of life and laughter. I was with Esme at The Carousel. She was standing in the office and I was there with her-waiting, watching- always in her shadow. Again that voice...

"Miss Thing, I'm talking to you...are you deaf on top of everything?"

I moved cautiously around Esme and came face to face with one of the largest people I had ever seen. However, his presence and his aura were much bigger than his size. He sat there- round and suspicious- peering at me with an interest I had never seen before. Before I could answer, Esme stepped in front of me pushing me further into the background...to wait and watch...as always.

"Ay, Francisco, you're so funny. How could he ever do drag with that nose?" Esme laughed. A great, roaring laugh at my expense...as always.

Francisco snapped his head and looked Esme directly in the eye.

"Oh miss thing, don't try it. I have known you for nearly 20 years and you should know by now that when I say someone has potential, they have potential. I saw it in you when no one else did. Don't laugh at him because one day, he may be laughing at you."

I was stunned. I had never heard anyone silence Esme that way. She was a Goddess. People simply did not challenge her. But I could tell instantly that something was different. This person was not your typical fag and everyone knew it...especially Esme.

"Do you speak?" He asked.

"I speak. And no I have not done drag."

"Well you should," he said, "and if you ever want to try it, I will help you."

"I don't know" I stammered. "I never really…."

"You should do it…you would be beautiful. You're so small and petite and you have great bone structure. Don't listen to anyone else. Listen to what I'm telling you…They don't want you to be beautiful. I do."

He was very dramatic when he spoke. Intense facial expressions and grand gestures with his hands.

"Why?" I asked.

"Because that's what I do," he said simply.

***

My friendship with Frank began very quickly. Like Ruben, I loved him immediately. He was funny, loud, so gay…. I finally began to relax. I became more confident and comfortable with myself…in my skin. But more importantly, I began to care less and less about what people thought. Frank taught me that. He would say,

"People don't think your straight miss thing…so stop trying to butch it up. You just come off looking more ridiculous. You will find that people respect you more if you just be yourself…and when you're ready, you're going to know that YOU may be someone very different than you expected."

Frank was like a God to me and I hung on his every word. He was a master at everything he did. He could make anything from pumpkin pie to an elaborate evening gown. All the queens would come to his house to be fitted for this and that. And I would sit watching…waiting…always waiting for my turn. He would watch me watching him…them…

"Miss Thing," he snapped. "When are you going to do drag?"

"I don't know."

"You do know that it is always more attractive to be young and beautiful don't you? I have no plans on dressing you when your grand-ma Moses. Decide please!"

"But my parents…"

"Girl, your parents will live…that which does not kill them will only make them stronger…Do you want to be a girl?"

I paused. I had never really had to answer that question before. My conversation with Celeste came flooding back to me. That day I had confided in her and she had told me that one day I was going to have to make a choice…Happiness or Bust!

I looked at Frank long and hard. Another one of the original old school Tampa queens Tameka Love was there too, waiting for my reply. She sighed very dramatically and said "Well?"

It was a life changing moment.

"Yes, I do."

CHAPTER 7

The Silicone came first. "We have to get you started, Frank said. Just a little in the face to build the cheekbones. You don't need much. After all we don't want you looking freakish…just a little apple…to give you that Snow White effect."

The Hormones came second- "Time to tell Your Mother." Frank sang joyously.

Telling Mom was considerably easier than I expected. She was hurt. I could see it in her eyes. But she put her arms around me and told me that she loved me and that she would always love me. I was her baby. I never felt closer to my mother than I did on that day. She left for awhile and when she came back she had a little balloon that said I love you on it. I still have that balloon somewhere…and I will always remember how good it felt to be honest with the one person I feared telling most. I felt liberated. My sister was easy too…she was too wrapped up in her own drama at the time to be worried about mine. She kissed me and said "Whatever makes you happy." My stepfather? I surprised him on father's day with the news. He had always hated me…now he had a reason to. Fuck him.

The hormones began to take effect over the next few months. Not one to be left behind, my friend Ruben began taking hormones too and he was developing much faster than I was. He always had a beautiful head of hair but now it was even more lustrous. His body was starting to take shape…small breasts were growing and he was now insisting we call her Lissette. Well, I thought, you will not be the only one. I upped my doses and before I knew it, my skin had changed, my hair was growing and my breasts- well they weren't. I consulted an expert- Frank. Frank suggested silicone treatments.

"Sometimes you have to build on what you're given. You may not grow big breasts from the hormones. You're a small, skinny person. You will be lucky to achieve an A cup."

"An A cup?" I screamed. "No way- I want to have breasts like Esme."

"Well then- start pumping...and while you're at it, you really should think of a name. You're much too feminine now to have people calling you by your boy's name."

"I haven't thought about it. What do you think?"

"Something exotic, Frank said, like you."

I thought about all of the beautiful classic film stars like Marilyn, Rita Hayworth, and Raquel Welch...And suddenly decided I would take the name of one of the most beautiful women I had ever seen on screen...And with the grand authority of a tried and true fairy Godmother, Frank clasped his hands together and exclaimed...

"I love it! From here on out- you will be...Sophia."

CHAPTER 8

Becoming Sophia was easier than I expected. I had always been very feminine but having a name to match my appearance just made it all the more real. My relationships with my gay friends were rapidly becoming the center of my universe. Nothing else seemed important. They pushed me further, faster than I could have ever pushed myself. Under their tutelage, I wasn't just becoming a woman, I was believing I was one.

"Not too fast" Frank would say. "You still have a lot to learn. Don't jump the gun."

"What's next?" I pleaded.

"Give it time" he replied.

But I was relentless. When Frank left for Miami to sponsor Victoria Mandrell for the Ms. Gay Universe Pageant I begged him to take me.

"I want to go in drag" I told him.

"You will not make your big debut at The Ms. Universe Pageant. Some of the most beautiful queens in the state will be there. You're not ready for that. Come with me…sit in the audience. Learn."

"But Frank…"

"Sophia"

So again I went…to watch…always watching…waiting for my turn. The girls were beautiful and though my transformation was nowhere near as advanced as most of the contestants in the pageant, I vowed then and there that I would not be a show queen. You see, my plans were much too big for suburbia. I wanted more. Lip synching was not a part of my plan.

I returned to Tampa with Frank who insisted I continue to consider performing as an option.

"I'll think about it." I promised.

Meanwhile, I continued to make the rounds of nightclubs and late night parties- often alone. Frank rarely went out- he was always busy at The Carousel. Lissette was always somewhat of a homebody and really didn't like to go out during the week. I found a fellow reveler in the sexy, sweet, sometime dancer/ sometime drag queen Ricardo. Ricardo or "Ricky" as I called him became my new partner in crime. My mother loved him because he was charming and handsome and because he truly loved my mother. He knew everyone and everyone knew him. As a result, I got into every nightclub in town even though I was too young including the ultimate club for an up and coming queen like myself- Rene's. Rene's was the birthplace of drag if you believed the hype. Home to the most beautiful female impersonators in the world. Esme had performed here but had been banished for "attitude problems." But the rest of the beauties were still there including the black Barbie doll, Lakesha Lucky, Esme's idol. From the moment I made it past the door, I knew I had come home. My look up to this point was very androgynous and Ricky still called me by my boy's name. He insisted upon it.

"Until you come out as a girl- that means, hair, make-up, the whole kit and caboodle- I will not call you Sophia."

For weeks I went back with him. I watched Lakesha, Bobbi Lake, and Tiffany Arreagus, all the greats…and I didn't just watch and wait. I watched and I learned. They each had that special something that made them different and equally impressive. I wanted to know how they had developed it.

"Your still young," Ricky would say, "But something tells me that when you find yourself, we'll all be in for the shock of the century. You will be beautiful- possibly the most beautiful ever- there is no doubt in my mind. All the doubt lies there." Ricky pointed to my temple as if to signify that my best trick would not be achieving greatness but finding a way to overcome the demons and insecurities that plagued me. He could be so wise. Not bad for a Puerto Rican drag queen with a drug habit. Call me crazy but needless to say, I loved him immediately.

CHAPTER 9

"Girl, I won." The voice that woke me at three in the morning on my private line at my parent's house was excited and a bit inebriated.

"What?"

"I won Miss Key West." It was Ricky

"Girl it's three in the morning. I have a bad headache."

"Oh you have a bad attitude" he said. "Listen, we have to be back here in a week. It will be a blast. You'll love it."

"I can't miss anymore work. They will fire me." I tried to protest.

"So, you barely work now...it'll be worth it."

"My mom..." I began.

"You let me worry about your mother. I'll be home in a couple of days. Get packing."

"Oh well...all right."

I decided it simply was not worth it to argue with him. He was in Syreeta Montiel mode- that was Ricky's alter drag ego. I would attempt to reason with him face to face when he got home. Problem was, HE didn't come home- SHE did. By the time Ricky returned to Tampa he was in full-tilt Miss Key West High Drag. Well you know what happened next- three days later, I was jobless, packed and driving my little blue Nissan Sentra across the state to experience all Key West had to offer including someone named Liza. I was 18 years old.

CHAPTER 10

It's way too early to explain the dynamic, eccentric, beautiful wild child-woman named Liza. In fact, my first encounter with her that summer in Key West provided no clues as to the importance that she would come to play in my life years later. Ricky and Liza were childhood friends and I had heard a lot about her, especially from him. Liza didn't work and that worked out very well for her if you know what I mean. She was fashionable, sexy, beautiful and smart as a whip. She lived in a beautiful condo with a view of the Atlantic and Ricky advised me that was our first stop on this Key West adventure.

"I have to pick something up." He said.

"What?"

"A little something," he said with a smile. "Oh God, did I tell you about Vidal? He's a gorgeous model that fell in love with me when I won Miss Key West. Wait till you meet him."

I rolled my eyes as if to say I KNEW IT. First Esme, now Ricky. When would it be my turn? Who would love me?

"Oh I can't wait," I said sheepishly.

"What's your problem Miss Thing?"

Before I could answer him he was frantically maneuvering me down Duval Street- the main through fare of the tiny little village of Old Town Key West. I couldn't believe what I was seeing. Gay couples, everywhere. Holding hands, kissing. Right there in front of God and everyone. Suddenly my petty jealousy went right out the window.

It was hot and sticky but the temperature seemed just perfect to me. The atmosphere was heady and intoxicating. I looked at Ricky. He flashed me that all knowing look of his.

"I knew you would love it," he said.

We pulled into the building Liza called home. At the time it was one of the grandest residences in The Keys.

We took the elevator up. When she threw open the front door she was everything I expected. She was a larger than life woman. The first real woman I had ever seen like that. She was dressed fabulously simple…jeans, a top…but the way she wore it spoke volumes about the kind of woman she was. She had a glass of champagne in her hand. The apartment was large and open with a view of the ocean.

"Hi Baby," she exclaimed. She had the biggest smile I had ever seen. She seemed so full of life. Again my insecurity got the best of me. I hid shyly behind Ricky. And much in the same sense a shark can sense fear, I felt her size me up and tire of me before she even had a chance to meet me. Without saying a word to me, she took Ricky by the hand, led him into the bedroom and shut the door. I settled onto the sofa to wait…again.

CHAPTER 11

After leaving Liza's, we headed to where we would be staying. The Atlantic Shores Hotel and Resort was a clothing optional hotbed of fabulous gay decadence. It was also a magnet for bi curious men which was great for me because my long hair and pretty, androgynous look was a perfect combination for men that liked both males and females. I wasn't even in the room when a rugged little redneck walked by, sizing me up. He was with an older woman. I wondered who she was but learned just moments later when he said in an accent as thick as Mississippi mud pie,

"Look Mama, he's so pretty for a boy."

Ricky collapsed -bags and all- into laughter.

"Girl, you did it," he screamed. "You converted your first confused straight man."

I couldn't help but laugh. Being with Ricky in that place- at that moment- was exhilarating. I felt free and beautiful. From that moment on, Key West became a part of my soul. A place I would return to time and time again, in good times as well as bad. But that moment on the steps of Atlantic Shores with Ricky always remained my definitive Key West memory. In many ways he made that moment. He was the moment. That was part of Ricky's charm, his magic. He wanted everything to be perfect for everyone. Everyone else came first...especially the people he loved most. I was one of those very special people for him. He truly was happy that someone had paid attention to me. It didn't just amuse him. It made him truly happy because he saw how happy I was that someone had finally noticed me and only me. I saw that when I looked in his eyes. Sad, kind eyes full of life and loss.

"You have a lot to learn, Girlie," he said. It was a statement that came from nowhere- possibly rooted in wisdom.

I don't think even he knew why he said it at that precise moment. I looked at him, long and hard.

"You're going to teach me," I said. I meant it.

"Let the games begin," he said.

***

The night began innocently enough. We met up with Vidal who was as beautiful as Ricky said. Vidal loved me immediately. He was a model and photographer who had been born and raised in Key West.

"You should do drag," he said within five minutes of meeting me. "I just photographed Dana Douglas for Miss Universe. I would love to photograph you with a green feather boa wrapped around your body and your hair piled high on top of your head."

His mannerism's reminded me of Frank. He was very animated and dramatic. I loved him too. We had dinner on Duval and decided to head to the infamous Copa for drinks afterwards. I had really pulled out all the stops tonight and was reveling in the attention. My naturally curly hair was wild from being in the sun all day. I was tanned and wearing my best half-drag. We arrived at The Copa and started pounding shots of tequila. Vidal didn't drink at the time but that was okay because Ricky and I were drinking enough for all of us. Before I knew what was happening, my spin on the dance floor was turning into a free fall. Ricky grabbed my arm and steered me to the restroom- The Women's of course.

"Miss Thing," he snapped, "This is the club that sponsored me in Miss Key West. You're underage and as drunk as a skunk. You have got to get a hold of yourself."

I laughed but knew he was serious. He was fuming. Apparently, I had snuck a few more drinks in and he was not amused. He knew he had to do something and fast. I was falling. If the club knew he had blatantly given alcohol to a minor, he could have been stripped of his Miss Key West title which was going to provide a hefty portion of his income over the next year.

Ricky pulled a small vial out of his pocket and poured a dime sized pile of white powder onto the spoon.

"Here, take this." He commanded.

I could feel my eyes starting to shut. I felt sick.

"What is it?" I asked.

"It's coke. It'll snap you out of this. Take it. Snort it back fast."

Visions of Michelle Pheiffer in Scarface came flooding back to me.

"How glamorous," I said. I took the first hit, then another.

The coke had its intended effect. I snapped back to attention. I loved it. Think Kristin Dunst in Interview With The Vampire. That first taste of blood.

"I want more," I said.

Ricky took a hit and put the vial back in his pocket.

"No," he said imperiously, "Go back to the room. I'm going with Vidal."

I walked alone down Duval to the hotel. I felt...wired and not ready for bed. As luck would have it, the rugged little redneck from earlier was standing outside his room, without his mother.

"Hey pretty boy," he said with a smile.

"Hey," I said shyly.

"I've been waiting for you..."

"Really? Why?" I asked.

"Cause I have something for you...if you want it."

I thought about it for a moment. This was a complete stranger. I didn't know him from Adam. I mean this man could have been a serial killer. In my somewhat paranoid state, he even looked a bit like one. There was only one logical thing to do. I followed him into his room and we drank and fucked until the sun came up. He turned out to be perfectly normal aside from the whole mother thing. You see, she was passed out in the bed next to us. And keeping quiet wasn't so easy.

CHAPTER 12

On the way back to Tampa several days later, Ricky told me to pick up the speed.

"Why?"

"Because I think it's time you made your big debut." He replied

"What do you mean?"

"I mean, that you are doing talent night at David's and you better press the gas because it starts at midnight."

"Talent night?"

Ricky gave a look…a long curious look. Then spoke very slowly and very dramatically as any drag queen would have done when trying to get their point across…

"Aren't you the one who said it's time? That we are all holding you back? Well, now's your chance."

"But I haven't talked to Frank…and he's the only one who can paint me. I'm still unsure of the makeup…"

He cut me off.

"Nonsense. Frank is not the only one who can paint you. I am quite capable of painting you just as good if not better."

"Are you sure Ricky?"

"I've never been more sure of anything in my life. It's time."

We arrived in Tampa at 10:30 pm and went right into overdrive. Ricky started my make-up. A master at what he knew it didn't take him long. The make-up wasn't drag which I liked. It was, however, pure stage. Think Vegas showgirl. The hair came next. Pieces of hair, extensions and mixed into my own long locks for a Julia Roberts Pretty Woman effect- Very long, very curly. When I looked at myself in the mirror, I was happy with the results. Not bad for a little boy with a little silicone. The body we faked but faked brilliantly. The dress was a black, skintight Contempo number and very then. Looking back, I can honestly say I was not the Goddess they called me later, but I had a confidence about me. I believed I was pretty. Ricky did too. The confidence I exuded was apparent and often came across as arrogance, even at that young age. But for the one's who WANTED me to be pretty, the excitement over my debut was contagious.

When I stormed the club that night, I moved through the crowd as though I was the one they had come to see.

The strange feeling inside- a mix of happiness, apprehension, insecurity- propelled me past friends, strangers and the people I like to refer to as "frenenemies" the ones who cheer you on publicly but can't wait to see you fall flat on your face. The gay world is full of them but Tampa...Tampa is where they live and breed. No city in the world can match it for all out bullshit and backstabbing hypocrites and every single one of them was in the house that night. I could feel Ricky's hand on the small of my back. He knew I was nervous.

"Don't worry honey, I'm here. No one's going to fuck with you. Eat up the scene. This is your moment."

I could see Frank standing by the bar. He gave me a big hug and told me I looked beautiful. He meant it. But I could also see that he was not amused by Ricky's sudden intrusion into his universe. I was his creation. There had always been a love/hate between the both of them. But they both loved me and for one night they put aside their animosity and began to prepare me.

"You need more gloss," Frank said.

"Your stage name will be Rachel. Sophia will be your real name but Rachel will be your stage name because you remind me a bit of Rachel Santoni," Ricky said.

I looked at them both. "Do I really have to go on stage and do drag?" I asked.

Then Frank said something very wise that I'll never forget. He said,

"No you don't have to. But can you think of a better way to build your courage? If your going to be a woman- a real woman- how are you ever going to walk down the street with straight people when you cant even get up on stage in front of a bunch of fags? This is crunch time miss thing. It's now or never. You wanted your chance. Here it is."

I walked out on that stage and I gave that number all I had. A slow, sad ballad that seemed to go on forever. My knees were shaking but I walked and mimicked the movements of my idol, Esme. It was all I knew how to do. But when it was over, I was first runner up in that little talent show and I had won a bottle of champagne. I celebrated with the two people who believed in me- Ricky and Frank. And that night...we laughed, we danced...And everyone had a friend and all was right in the world.

CHAPTER 13

By the time my debut had ended, I knew I could never step foot into a club out of drag again. Even though I was still unsure about a career as a performer, I knew I had crossed the line. I was not going to be a "boy-queen." I would, from this moment on, be identified as Sophia. That meant, in a nutshell, leaving home. I had lived at home all of my life. It was time for a change. My stepfather would never stand for my doing drag in his house.

I hated him anyway. Our arguments were becoming more and more heated. So as luck would have it, an old boyfriend offered me a place to stay. Ken had been a fling from The Carousel but we turned out to truly like each other and remained friends. He was very handsome, ex-military and a true and generous friend in my young life. By the time we moved in together, our "moment" had come and gone but he still understood my need to break away and he was more than willing to let me have his spare room. That's when everything went into fifth gear. I upped the hormones, began experimenting with "daytime drag." Because I was no longer home and Ken was more than supportive of my choices, I was able to put the gas on and continue with my transformation.

I was able to grab a new job to facilitate my new living arrangement. How long it would last with my nighttime excursions taking top priority in my life, I didn't know. But I went out every night- in drag- and woke up every morning and went to work. It was working for me. Going out as a woman allowed me an opportunity that had never been afforded me as an underage boy. The one club in town that had always been strictly off limits was Tracks. Even Esme was unable to get me through the door. But the moment I showed up in drag, the doors magically opened. I had carte blanche. Suddenly everyone wanted to know who I was. My look was dramatic and exotic but much more realistic than a lot of the girls on the scene at the time. Along with the show queens, there were several other beauties vying for the spotlight- Connie, the oriental Barbie was definitely the "Girl of the Moment." Like an Asian Edie Sedwick in a modern day Factory, she paraded through Tracks in scanty costumes and bikinis. Connie was very good friends with my old friend Ruben who by now was living as Lissette. As a result, we became close and the three of us ran rampant through the streets of Ybor City, Tampa's version of Bourbon Street. All of us were quite pretty in our own unique ways and it was amazingly easy to fool the boys. They practically fell over themselves to talk to us. Though we were frightened at first, we loosened up and before we knew what was happening, we had become quite confident in our abilities to attract unsuspecting straight men. The hard part was keeping their hands from running crazy on your body once you got a rise out of them- Not an easy thing to do when you have a dick shoved down your throat in the back seat of a car. Looking back, I realize what a dangerous game we were playing. But we were young and having fun and what a high it gave us to know that some hot straight guy honestly thought we were women.

And on this went for well over a year. We continued honing our skills as women, as actresses and as sexual seductresses. My hair got longer, my body developed and my ego began to get completely out of control. Everyone and I mean everyone told me I was beautiful. Sometimes they said it twice to make sure I heard it. What they didn't know was that I wasn't just hearing it- I was processing it, digesting it and believing it. The power I felt was nothing compared to the power I would come to experience years later when my look really came together. But at the moment it was every bit as seductive. I began jockeying for the spotlight. Lissette -as beautiful as she was- was always very shy and not interested in being the alpha queen. But I decided that I would not stand in Connie's shadow any longer. Something had to give…The gay scene was completely played out for us. If we were going to stay friends we would have to evolve. We would have to make the jump into the straight world…and into the straight clubs.

CHAPTER 14

The straight Tampa club scene was definitely not prepared for what happened next. With all the subtlety of a train wreck, the three of us exploded onto the party scene. Make no mistakes, we were beautiful. More beautiful than most of the women and everyone knew it. That was a good thing and a bad thing. Good because the boys loved us, bad because the girls didn't. It took several months for them to get used to the idea that we weren't going anywhere. We were at every club, every after hours, the before and in between hours. Some people were immediately cool. The boys were always easy but concealing their feelings from their friends became a kind of tricky situation that many of them raised to an absolute art form. The girls were haters- plain and simple. At that moment in time we were dealing with not too cute, not so fashionable females who worked at The Food Court and then tried to give attitude at the clubs later. Well, my days of being Miss Congeniality were definitely over. I simply refused to take their shit. I checked every single one of them. I was becoming quite anti-female at the time. It would be another year or so before I would meet the beautiful strippers that would forever change my life and my perception of women in general.

One ace in the hole we had was Hector Adorno. Hector was a friend, closer to Connie at the time than to any of us. He was fabulous and gay and everyone- straight and gay- loved him. He came from a family of thugs but if they loved you they loved you. They protected you. Hector was a permanent fixture in the straight scene.

No one fucked with him. He began to accompany us, introduce us and make sure that no one else fucked with us either. Fuck with him- Fuck with his Family. That was the motto and everyone knew it. Things began to change. Suddenly girls weren't quite as ready to be catty and the so-called tough boys- the one's that pretended to laugh at you in front of their friends then asked you to fuck them up the ass in private- well they weren't laughing anymore. Social acceptance was Hectors lasting gift to us. Unfortunately, he came bearing other gifts as well. Now before I proceed, let me say one thing. I was an adult, as were Connie and Lissette and the choices we made were completely our own. No one forced me to make those choices. I made them because I wanted to. Because I thought it was cool, hip, glamorous and because everyone else was doing it. I blame no one but myself for what came next.....

CHAPTER 15

In order for you to understand the choices I made and the turn that my life began taking, you must understand my relationship with a very addictive substance. My addiction to cocaine began relatively innocent enough. A bump here, a bump there. Ultimately, the drug would allow me to make choices for myself I may not have necessarily made had I not had a line of coke to get me through it. In the mid nineties, everyone I knew was doing blow. It was "the thing to do." All the cool people- the crowd you wanted to be a part of- they were doing it most of all. It all began at The Bridge Club. Everyone at The Bridge was doing it or dealing it or both. I bought my first package from a queen that everyone knew all too well. It was complete shit. I tried again- this time with someone with a little more credibility. I had been drinking white wine all night. The first bump re-energized me. About 10 minutes later, I went back to the bathroom for another- ten minutes later, another bathroom trip...and so on and so on until the coke was gone and the sun was coming up outside. Hector, Connie and I stood outside The Bridge trying to figure out what our next move was.

"Let's buy some more," Hector suggested.

"I don't have any more money," Connie said.

"Neither do I," I said.

"Well great!" Hector said. "Then I guess we can just go home."

At that moment a little fag came running up to us.

"You guys want to go to an after hours at my house? About fifteen people."

I was immediately game. Connie hit it home. Hector said he was going home if we couldn't find blow. So I alone followed the feminine little fag back to his modest place in North Tampa. The driveway was already swarmed with cars. People were milling about outside waiting for him to get home…mostly gay men but some girls, one sad little queen who kept looking at me as though I had three heads. I seemed to be the guest of honor at this little soiree because everyone- most of whom I didn't know- wanted to be near me, to touch me.

"Hey Girl, wanna bump?"

I turned and looked into the most beautiful brown eyes I had ever seen. Pause collectively and imagine this-

Tall, dark and handsome. Rugged, tattooed bad boy with chiseled features and a hard, lean body. He was quite simply the most beautiful man I had ever seen.

"Sure."

I followed him into the house, into the bathroom and he locked the door. From his pocket he produced a very large bag of coke- a very large bag. He handed it over to me.

"Here", he said, take what you want."

I was about to stick my nail in the bag when he stopped me.

"No, not like that. Let me show you."

He scooped two large bumps from the bag, laid them out on the counter and cut it into two very fat lines. Then he pulled a twenty out of his pocket, rolled it up and snorted one. I was mesmerized. He handed me the twenty.

"Now you." He said.

I did the same. Then he smiled at me. A beautiful, lingering smile.

"You're a very sexy girl." He said.

Then he kissed me on the cheek, walked out of the bathroom, talked to the host for about a minute and walked out.

"Who was that?" I asked.

Our host smiled, very well aware of the effect the man had had on me.

"That was the candy man," he replied.

CHAPTER 16

"Let's get some coke." I suggested.

It was late Friday night and Lissette and I were on our way to Yucatan Liquor Stand, the straight hot spot of the moment.

"I don't really like coke. Let's just stick to drinking." she replied.

I could always count on her to be the voice of reason. Reluctantly, I agreed and we headed down the interstate toward the club. We were dressed incredible. Lissette had a stunning black dress on which showed off her incredible cleavage- I opted for a skintight white dress and white go-go boots and tried something new with my hair- I pulled it straight back into a tight bun at the nape of my neck. It was a look Esme had perfected. As luck would have it, the look also worked very well on me. It was too severe a look for most queens to pull off but Frank insisted I try it.

"I knew it would work. That is a true testament to your beauty and the features of your face," Frank said before we left the house.

Yucatan was slammed. We walked in the door and the crowd parted. I heard the dj say loudly over the speaker,

"Watch out boys, here come Thee Dollhouse girls."

Thee Dollhouse was Tampa's premier strip club which by coincidence happened to be next door to The Yucatan. A lot of Thee Dollhouse girls hung out at Yucatan and Lissette and I were quite pleased that we had been mistaken for upscale strippers. It didn't get any classier than that, right? The boys were going wild. We were in rare form that night. Drinks came freely- from bartenders, from various men. The girls were seething. God, how I loved to make haters of them. I used to say,

"I don't care if I walk into the room and every person in the room knows I'm a man. The one thing they'll know by the time I leave is that I was definitely the most beautiful woman in the place."

We danced all night- often all over each other which really drove the boys wild. It was one of those perfect nights.

"Lets go to Tracks and see what's going on," I said.

"Okay." Lissette agreed.

On our way toward Ybor we stopped for gas. A minute later a white Ferrari- a new white Ferrari- pulled up beside us. I rolled my window down. The man driving was about thirty five. He was preppy and very handsome.

"What's up beautiful?" he asked.

I smiled. "What's up with you?"

"You don't want to know." he replied.

"Don't be so sure."

"You want to go for a ride?"

"Can I bring my sister?"

"Sure, she'll have to sit on your lap." He smiled as though the very idea of her on my lap stirred a fantasy deep within him.

I looked at Lissette. She was game. I suggested she leave her car at Yucatan. We could come back for it later.

We hopped in the car. He smiled, quite pleased with himself.

"Where to?" He asked.

"My house," I replied.

We sped off toward the apt I shared with Ken near USF, a good twenty minutes from Yucatan. On the way, I played with him intensely. My tongue on his neck, my hand pulling at this zipper. I could feel him growing.

"Baby, you are going to drive me crazy," he moaned. Lissette got in on the act as we sped 120 miles down the freeway. The car swerved but we kept right on playing. The music was loud- The Doors- I felt incredible.

It seemed like forever, but we finally made it home. The minute he was in the door, I had his pants off. He tore Lissette's dress down and worked her breasts while I sucked his cock. The threesome went on until we were tired- we, as in me and Lissette- then we politely asked him to leave.

"But I can come more than once," He protested. "I'm not done."

I smiled and kissed him on the cheek.

"We are," I replied

The sweet but stern look on my face came across quite clearly. He got up and pulled his pants on.

"Can I get your number?" He asked.

"Why?"

"Cause I would like to get together again."

"I don't think that would be a good idea." I replied still smiling sweetly.

Confused, he kissed me on the cheek and walked out the door. Lissette seemed as confused as he was.

"Girl, are you crazy? He was hot and has a Ferrari!"

I looked at her with a very bored look in my eye.

"Yes, but he has a five inch cock with absolutely no girth and you know how I feel about those."

That night after washing off our make-up, Lissette and I sat up listening to music well into the morning, laughing and talking and becoming the kind of friends you only make once in a lifetime.

CHAPTER 17

We finished up the last few weeks of summer with more clubs, more boys, more parties, more boys, the beach, more boys. Lissette and I became running partners. We were always together. It was an innocent time in our lives. Lissette wasn't into coke so my preoccupation with finding the drug subsided for awhile. We just drank when we went out and enjoyed being young and beautiful and desirable. Ken had told me that he would be giving up his apartment in Tampa and moving to Gainesville to be near his new boyfriend James. That meant I would either have to find a new place I could afford alone, a new roommate or go home to my parents house. My job was on shaky ground as I was constantly calling in sick because of my late night partying. It didn't help that my appearance had become more and more feminine. I decided to have a chat with my mom. I took her to lunch at a little place we used to like in old west Tampa. She was a little shocked at how feminine I looked but was supportive.

"Come home," she said.

"Mom, I'm not going to change my way of life. I am going to become a woman."

"Come home," she said again.

I hated my step father but loved my mother dearly. She was trying to get her drinking under control. She wasn't feeling all that well.

"I miss you," she said.

"Okay mama," I said, "I'll come home."

And I did.

Things got off to a shaky start at home. My stepfather and I clashed immediately. He ignored me most of the time- I did the same. It worked most of the time. When it didn't, you would have thought World War Three was underway. My mom was mediator but my personality was and has always been extremely confrontational. I am a fighter, a scrapper. I don't back down from anyone. The hormones effected me in strange ways in the early years. If he called me a faggot, I called him a lousy, no-good motherfucker. He learned to avoid me. The pure venom in my tone, the hatred in my eyes- It scared even my mother. I was on the other side of the house and re connected my private line so I did my best to avoid him when he was home. I only went into the kitchen if I really needed something. I did spend as much time as I could with my mom but often times we clashed as well. The work situation was no better than my living arrangement. Eventually, they got sick of me calling in sick and fired me. Great thing about being fired and back at home was that I could collect unemployment and spend most of it on partying...and I did. I went out every night of the week and I do mean every night. During the day I'd go to the mall or the beach...wherever I could find the boys. I met my first serious boyfriend shortly after. Victor was a soft-spoken, very handsome Cuban male. Extremely sexual and extremely sexy. We had a great time when we were together and his family was very cool and completely accepting of me. Victor also had a small coke problem and I was more than happy to party with him. With him, I finally experienced the true effect of the drug. The never ending, stay out all night, I want more effect that would become such an integral part of my life. That was because he always had the best shit- not the baking soda they sold in the clubs. I loved it. I wanted it all the time- at least every time I went out which was every night. I started partying with him and without him. The gay clubs were a perfect place for me to find it and half the time the dealers just gave it to me.

"You're too beautiful to pay," they would say.

I took it every time. I didn't even see it coming. Cocaine also opened the door for more experimentation. When I couldn't fall asleep at night after partying, I used tranquilizers and sleeping pills to cut the high. This was an everyday occurrence. My mother wasn't stupid. She knew what I was doing and she would explode. She was worried and pissed. I retaliated by spending more and more time away from home. But know matter where I was, I called her every day to let her know that I was okay. She appreciated that. One night, Victor decided again to go out with his brother and told me to do something with Lissette. I called her up to see what she was doing.

"Girl, I'm going to a rave. It's incredible. Connie and I went last week. There are boys everywhere and everyone's doing X and the music is amazing. You have to experience it. I can't explain it."

"What's X?" I asked.

"Ecstasy," she replied. It's a pill. It makes you feel wild and sexy. Everyone's doing it."

"I'll just get some coke," I said.

"No, you have to be on the same level as everyone else. It's a group experience. I can't explain it. Trust me."

I thought about it for a moment. I would have preferred coke but if Lissette was going to do it, I guess I would try it to.

"All right, get me one. What time does it start?"

"It starts at three in the morning and goes till twelve in the afternoon."

An all night rave party. I had heard stories about the rave scene. Some good. Some bad. I was about to make up my own mind and I would never be the same again.

CHAPTER 18

That night, I took special care to look even more beautiful than usual. I poured my tight ass into a skimpy little dress and a pair of boots. I looked hot. Lissette agreed. We set off for Hammerjax, the downtown club where the rave was being held. The line was around the corner but Lissette assured me that Connie would be waiting at the door to get us in immediately. She was. The beefy security guard at the door gave Connie a kiss and waved us through. The club was still cleaning up from earlier so the rave had not actually started.

"The only people allowed in right now are the crème de la crème," Connie said. "I have a lot of friends that you have to meet. Hector will probably be here. Karen and Stacy are really cool...and you have to meet Sierra. She's absolutely stunning."

There were about thirty people inside. Most of the girls were absolutely beautiful, dressed to kill. The men were hot with amazing bodies and perfect faces.

"Why haven't I ever seen any of these people out?" I asked.

"The girls are all strippers- mostly Dollhouse and Mons- so they're normally working when the rest of us are out," Connie replied. "The boys are here for them. But don't worry, everyone is cool and you will have a good time. I'll go get our pills."

Lissette and I found a spot at the bar and waited for Connie to get back. I could feel a knot in my stomach. There was a lot going on inside of my head. I was a little more than nervous about taking the pill. I don't know why. I just was. A minute later, the house lights went off and the front door opened. The masses started to enter the club. The music started. The music was not your typical dance music. The beat was much faster, more hypnotic with continual breaks and soaring female vocals. It was the most danceable dance music I had ever heard. I began to move.

"Lissette, let's dance," I said.

"Wait till we take our pill," she replied.

At that moment, Connie appeared at our side, an excited look on her face.

"I have already taken my pill. Here."

She handed us two very large pills that she referred to as wafers.

"Take a half only," Lissette instructed me. "Then save the other half for next time."

"Next time?" I asked.

Lissette smiled as if to say, there will definitely be a next time. I washed down half the pill with a bit of juice.

"Now what?" I asked.

"Now we wait," Lissette replied. "Twenty minutes...and then, pure heaven."

While we waited for the pill to take effect, Connie & Lissette began introducing me to a small group of people that seemed very cool. You have to remember, that the three of us were very used to the idea of people in the straight scene being indifferent and sometimes even rude to us. By comparison, these people immediately seemed like family. Hector had arrived with an entourage and they too embraced us. The mood in the club was very relaxed. Everyone seemed to be friendly. Complete strangers would walk by me and smile and touch my arm. Shirtless muscle boys I didn't know would kiss my hand or cheek as they passed. The women-everyone of them more beautiful than the last- stopped to tell me how beautiful I was and I could tell they meant it. The absence of alcohol and the fact that everyone seeded to be on the same high- X—heightened the feeling of euphoria and complete togetherness. It was like nothing I had ever experienced. I had almost forgotten about the pill, when all of a sudden, I felt it...

I can not explain the feeling that came over me the first time I did X. In the years that followed, I would do X hundred's of times and always feel incredible. But NEVER like that first time. That first time was amazing.

The rush that enveloped me was nothing short of startling. I have never felt more alive. I never felt better about myself or about life in general. It felt really fucking good. Better than that. Imagine a thousand simultaneous orgasm's- lights and music inside your very head, carrying you into the music, into the very beat and back again and those orgasm's continuing, never ending and every problem, every insecurity that ever plagued you- gone, never known. That is X. Now multiply it over and over again and you will have some idea of how it feels that very first time.

'Are you rolling yet?" Lissette asked. I could see by the look on her beautiful face that she was.

I couldn't even answer her. I just touched her hand and nodded my head.

"Don't walk away because the boys will be all over you. Stay with me," she instructed.

"Okay," I replied.

Lissette turned back to the bar to order another juice. For some odd reason, I just walked away and let the music propel me toward the dance floor. When I reached the floor, I noticed five hot guys- all shirtless- dancing with a very beautiful blonde girl.

"Dance with us," she called out smiling.

I joined them. I could feel the drug throughout my body. The boys were touching me as we danced. The girl was watching and smiling, encouraging them. I danced for what seemed like hours. One of the guys was especially attentive and he asked me if I wanted some juice or water. I nodded and he took me by the hand and steered me toward the bar. He was gorgeous. Tall and muscular with a rippling washboard stomach.

What's your name?" He asked.

"Sophia."

"I'm Robert. Your so beautiful."

"You too."

I could see Lissette on the other side of the bar.

"I need to grab my friend," I managed to say.

"No worries, I'll catch up with you. You want me to walk you over there?"

"No thanks, I'm good."

He bent down and kissed me softly on the lips. I smiled and made my way over to the other side of the bar where Lissette was waiting with a small group of beautiful people.

"Where the hell have you been?" She asked immediately.

"Dancing," I replied.

I took a sip of her juice. It felt like liquid gold inside my mouth. It was electric. The X continued to keep spinning inside of my body- there were moments of amazing highs and amazing lows- but not the kind of lows that one would find bleak or disenchanting. The lows were great too. . .just lazy moments in the high before it sent you spinning back up toward heaven. Connie was dancing on the bar. God, she was beautiful. More beautiful at that moment than I had ever remembered her. Suddenly she spotted someone in the crowd.

"Sierra!" She called.

Lissette snapped to attention as did Hector.

"Sophia. Wait till you see this girl," Lissette said. "She is beautiful."

The crowd parted and "this girl" was unlike any woman I had ever seen. At the moment, the X may have made her seem all the more unreal but even today, she remains the most beautiful woman I have ever seen standing in front of me. She was extremely exotic, to put it mildly. Dark straight hair framed hazel naturally cat-shaped eyes, full lips and high, perfect cheekbones. Her body was tight and muscular but completely feminine with amazingly large breasts that were obviously implants. She moved with flawless precision through the crowd, completely aware of her effect and of her power. People stepped back to watch her. Everyone seemed to know her or know of her or want to know her. I was transfixed. She was, quite simply, spellbinding.

"Sierra!" Connie called again.

Sierra looked up and smiled. Beautiful smile, radiant…. I was quickly losing my composure. She made her way through the crowd and gave Connie a kiss.

"Hey Girl," she said. Her voice was unique and melodious and while she spoke with Connie, she moved sexily, running her hands across her body, smiling as the X took hold of her, enjoying the music and the attention of all the eyes upon her. I stood riveted. She and Connie walked toward us. Sierra embraced Lissette.

"Sierra," Lissette said, "This is my best friend Sophia."

"Sophiaaaa," She smiled as she dragged out my name.

"You are the most beautiful woman I have ever seen," I said simply.

She smiled. "You are beautiful...very beautiful."

I smiled. Karen ran over to whisper in Sierra's ear and Sierra nodded, then pulled some money out of her purse. Then she looked at me and said,

"Want to dance?"

"Sure," I replied.

She took me by the hand and we made our way toward the dance floor. Everyone was watching. When she danced, she seemed even more ethereal. Something in the way she moved. She knew she was beautiful. She knew that everyone else knew it too. That was her power. Her confidence. She didn't try to be sexy. She was. It was within her. Some girls fake it and it's still sexy. But when you have IT- really have IT- it's something entirely different and she had IT in spades. We didn't say anything. She just watched me, watching her. We continued rolling and dancing and before I knew it, I had made a new friend.

"Let's go back," she suggested.

I followed her back to the bar. Everyone was laughing, having a great time. Everyone was beautiful, happy. I remember it like it was yesterday and yet it seems like a hundred years ago. That night, we danced and rolled until the sun came up. At various times throughout the course of the rave, we drifted apart- sometimes me & Sierra, Connie and Lissette, me & Karen, me and some hot boy- but we all ended up back in our little corner at the bar. As the sun came up outside, I thought of Victor, waiting for me back at his place. I looked at Lissette.

"I better go."

"Can you drive?" she asked.

"I can drive," I replied.

"Why don't you stay? We're all going back to Courtney's place later."

"I better get back to Victor."

They all kissed me goodbye and told me to be careful. It was such familial feeling. There was no pretension or cattiness about the way my new friends had behaved with me. They had openly welcomed me into their fold.

That night was just the beginning...and my new little circle was just a small part of the scene I would forever be associated with. But that night, I knew I had found the one place on earth where I finally felt completely and utterly free...

CHAPTER 19

The week went by pretty quickly. All the while, I daydreamed about The Rave. I had, many times over the week, taken out my half of X, inspected it, contemplated taking it but knew that rolling in my living room would not be cute. I would simply have to wait. By Thursday, I was itching for some fun. I decided to head out to Hammerjax alone and see what kind of trouble I could get into. Hammerjax was only slightly happening. Tracks was the place to go on Thursday's. It was straight night on Thursdays and everyone who was anyone went. I decided to have one drink at Hammerjax and then head to Tracks. Before I had a chance to order the drink, I felt someone brush up against me.

"Sophiaaaa." Again that voice, dragging my name. It was Sierra and again she looked incredible. She was wearing a pair of tight jeans and a tight, black cropped top. She was with Courtney and Karen. They all embraced me warmly.

"What's up?" They asked in unison.

"Just popped in for a drink." I replied.

"No one's here," Sierra said with a hint of disappointment. "Where do people go on Thursday's?"

"Tracks," I replied.

"But isn't that gay?" Karen asked.

"Not tonight, it's straight." I replied.

"That's right," Sierra said, "I forgot."

"Let's go," I said.

Courtney and Karen decided against it. They both had to work in the morning. Sierra said we would take her car and off we went in her brand new Lexus. As we drove, I noticed a stunning very large diamond on her ring finger.

"Are you married?" I asked.

"No…well sort of. I'm engaged to Bobby Brant, he owns one of the more popular strip clubs in town."

I couldn't help but stare at her. She was absolutely beautiful. I wasn't rolling. She was the real deal.

"How long have you been this way?" She asked.

"A few years," I replied.

"Do you do drag?" she asked.

"No," I replied. "What do you do?"

"Well, I used to dance. I still do occasionally. But Bobby doesn't really want me working at the club."

"Your beautiful." I said suddenly. I couldn't help myself. She smiled.

"Are you rolling?" she asked.

"No, are you?"

"A little," she replied. "I took a quarter piece. I don't want to get too fucked up."

Sierra looked at me as we drove.

"What?" I asked.

"Your very pretty," she said. "You and Connie and Lissette are really like beautiful girls."

"Thanks."

We pulled up outside of Tracks and the line was around the building. This time, I walked us through. I held tightly to her hand and watched as the crowd parted for us. Alone, I was dangerous enough. But with this girl at my side, I was literally explosive. Boys were doing double takes, triple takes, turning around completely and trying to catch up with us. The effect the two of us had on men when we were together was awe-inspiring. Two exotic beauties at the very center of everyone's attention. We danced for awhile, grabbed some drinks and basically just got to know each other a little better. She was nice, slightly guarded but nice. We flirted with the boys and before we knew it, the night was over.

"I better get you back to your car," she said, "I have to get home."

"I'll find my way back," I said.

"Are you sure?" she asked genuinely concerned.

"I'm sure. I'm on the prowl."

She smiled. There was something in that smile. I can't explain the effect she had on me. It wasn't sexual or spiritual. It was completely visual. I simply had never seen anyone quite like her. And somewhere inside of her, I saw myself.

"I had fun Sophia." She said. "I'll see you this weekend."

Then she turned and left the club and everyone in the immediate area, myself included, stopped to watch her go.

CHAPTER 20

The next afternoon, I called Lissette and begged her to go out. She pleaded, saying that she wanted to stay in and save her energy for The Rave the following evening. I was insistent and finally she gave in.

"But something low key," she said.

We agreed on Tracks. My relationship with Victor was unraveling quickly so going out with Lissette was no problem. He had already made plans with his brother. When we arrived at Tracks, we immediately went to the Quiet Bar. Tracks was the largest club in Tampa at the time. It had several large rooms and the Quiet Bar was the first bar you entered when you came into the club. We downed a couple of shots and moved on to the next room. As the shot took effect, Lissette , who would have gotten drunk on a shot of lemonade if you told her it was alcohol, decided she wanted to dance.

"I don't want to go out on the floor," I said. "Let's dance here."

As we danced, I noticed a hot guy at the bar, checking us out. He was very muscular, dark and handsome. His hair was absolutely beautiful- long and straight—all one length and cut to his chin. There was also something strangely familiar about him.

"Lissette, look at the guy at the bar."

She turned around.

"Hmmm…He's hot," she said.

"Let's go get another drink." I said.

We walked over to the bar and he smiled at me as we approached.

"Hey beautiful," he said.

"Hey."

"Remember me?" he asked.

When the strobe caught his face and I could finally see him clearly, I knew exactly who he was. My gorgeous "candy man" from the gay after hours party a few months before.

"How could I forget you?" I asked.

He seemed to like that answer. He bought us another round of shots and led us both to the dance floor. He was a great dancer. He moved sexily between the both of us. I ran my hands along his muscular, tattooed arms. The man was beautiful. He smiled, looking into my eyes.

"You are so beautiful," he whispered.

We danced all night. We drank. He had a lot to say but it was all very impersonal. Mostly small talk but somehow it still seemed relevant. There was something about this man I could not quite put my finger on. What I knew for sure was that I didn't just want to suck his cock or fuck his brains out- I wanted to know him. Really KNOW him.

"Do you have a girlfriend?" I asked.

Silence.

"Do you have...a boyfriend?

Silence.

"Maybe I have both," he replied. Suddenly his demeanor changed. He had a far away look in his eyes. His eyes were dark and sad yet heartbreakingly beautiful as though they had lived a thousand lives.

"I'm kind of trying to find...myself." he said quietly.

It was a very intimate moment between two complete strangers. I knew I had connected with him. But as quickly as the moment had come, it was gone. He brightened up.

"I have to go," he said. He kissed me on the cheek, kissed Lissette's hand and headed for the door.

"Wait!" I called after him. "That's it?"

He smiled. That incredible, perfect smile.

"Can I have your number?" I asked, against my better judgment.

He walked back toward me.

"I can't give you what you deserve right now. I've got too much going on."

"I'm not asking for a relationship or marriage. I just…want to see you."

"You will," he promised.

"You know we've been talking and dancing all night and you never even got my name." I said.

"Your name's Sophia," he replied. "I knew it the day I met you. But, I'm pretty sure you don't know my name."

I felt completely embarrassed. Had I really spent the entire evening with this man and neglected to ask his name? I started to laugh. He laughed too. God, his eyes were incredible. He kissed me again on the cheek and said "Catch you later beautiful."

"Are you going to tell me your name?" I asked.

He turned one last time.

"Charlie." he said.

Then he turned and walked out of my life for the second time. I was never the same. It would be several years before I saw him again but the man was always right there- inside of my head- never far from my thoughts. That one perfect man I couldn't keep or seduce or even know. I was 20 years old when I fell in love. I just didn't know it then.

CHAPTER 21

"The rave has moved. They're having a problem with Hammerjaxx so it's over at The Krush." Connie was on the phone with Karen getting the 411 as Lissette and I got ready.

"That sucks," I said.

"It'll still be fun. Do you have your pill?" Lissette asked.

"Is a frog's ass water-tight?" I asked and we both collapsed in laughter.

"I can't wait to roll," I said. I could feel the excitement, the sheer anticipation swelling up inside of me. I didn't realize it then, but I was at the very beginning of my addiction. Cocaine had opened the door for X. X would ultimately open the door for experimentation with everything else including acid, special K, painkillers, even heroin. But at that moment, it was just fun and games.

We arrived at the club at about 3:30 am and there was already a line forming. Connie got us to the front of the line where Sierra was waiting with Courtney and Karen and Karen's boyfriend Stacy. Everyone looked great.

Sierra was already rolling. I could see it in her cat eyes.

"I'm taking my roll now." I announced.

I took Sierra's bottled water and took a swig. The pill tasted horrible but I could have cared less.

"You look hot," Sierra said smiling.

"Thanks," I said, "You too."

"I know," she whispered mischievously.

Once inside, the music was intoxicating, pounding. The club was much larger than Hammerjaxx so there was more room to dance and more room to breathe. We decided to do a lap around the club first.

"See and be seen," Sierra would say.

'Come with me to the bathroom," Lissette demanded. "You have got to see the guy that just walked in there."

I followed her into the large open restroom. Take into consideration that in the early days of raving, most club restrooms were unisex. The Krush restroom had a large waiting room and twenty stalls in a separate area. The waiting room was filled with people waiting for a stall or just hanging out.

"Have you ever seen anything...like...ever?" Lissette was dumbfounded.

I followed her gaze. Leaning against the wall was a man that I can only describe as a Viking Barbarian God.

Probably 6'5, solid muscle, no shirt, perfect abs, blonde hair to his waist. He was striking but much more Lissette's type than my own. I liked them dark and handsome not blonde and pretty.

"I have never...I just..." Lissette continued to speak as eloquently as she could manage in her drug induced stupor. On the X, he must have seemed like Conan to her.

I smiled. She continued to stare at him but I found my gaze wandering toward the girl he was with. Talk about striking. She wasn't very tall but her look was dark, even a bit severe. Think Betty Page with a nineties twist.

She had a jet black china bob, small, pretty features and quite possibly the largest breasts I had ever seen in my life. She was wearing a skin-tight black velvet bodysuit and her body was nothing short of outrageous. He finally got his stall and as she waited, she noticed me too. She smiled. Again, I felt it. Sierra had done it. Now, this girl was doing it to. She was drawing me in. Her eyes were fixed on me. She didn't look away. I smiled and looked away uncomfortably. She kept staring at me. She was smiling- a half-smile really. Not quite friendly...more curious. I walked toward her. Her eyes never left me for a moment.

"Your really beautiful," she almost whispered it, as though it were a secret we shared.

"You are...amazing. I can't describe you." I replied.

"You don't have to try," she said. "I get it. I get you."

Those eyes burned right through me. I felt as though we had met somewhere before but knew that we hadn't.

She kept right on staring at me. That curious half smile.

"What's your name?" I asked.

"Dominique," she replied, "You are?"

"Sophia,"

"I saw you with Sierra." she said.

"Do you know Sierra?"

"Everyone knows Sierra. I work at Thee Dollhouse. I do know her." She replied. "She's very beautiful isn't she?"

She said it more like a statement than a question as though she clearly knew that Sierra was beautiful but wanted to hear my opinion anyway.

"Yes, she is," I said.

Again that half-smile.

"Yes, she is," she agreed.

There was a strange silence between us as we sized each other up. Conan returned. She introduced him.

"John, say hi to Sophia. She's my new friend. You'll be seeing a lot of her."

He smiled.

The roll was beginning to peak and she seemed even more larger than life. I couldn't stop staring at her. She knew that look in my eyes was chemically induced.

"I wont keep you from your roll Sophia...or your Sierra," she said. "Have fun."

Then she walked out with her Viking and that is how I met one of the women who became one of the key players in my life and in my transformation.

CHAPTER 22

If it seems like nothing else was going on in my life at this time other than drugs, sex and techno, it's because there wasn't. I wasn't working. I was spending absolutely zero time with my family which had grown to include an adorable nephew. I wasn't looking for work. I was just having fun. I was perfectly content with my life. I had broken up with Victor when he insisted I choose between him and raving. I fought with my family constantly about my partying but undeterred, raved on and continued rolling with my homeys. I was quickly becoming a legend in Tampa. Everyone was talking about *that really hot chick that used to be a guy.* Of course it helped that I was always surrounded by the hottest females in town and they in turn made sure that no one fucked with me. I was out every night and at every rave not just in Tampa but in Orlando as well. Dominique was quickly becoming my new best friend. After seeing each other a couple of more times, we had exchanged numbers and had begun hanging out on a regular basis. Her real name was Tish. Dominique was her stage name. She wasn't just hot in her own unique way- she was smart and quick witted and sexy and strange. I liked everything about her. She was the one who first suggested I kick it up a notch.

"There is no hotter accessory than a fine ass muscle boy," she said. "Gay, straight, friend, boyfriend, fuck buddy, whatever. When you walk into a club always have one or more with you, meeting you or leaving with you. That's what keeps them guessing. Don't ever be predictable. That's the best advice I can give you."

I took it to heart and found exactly what I was looking for at The Rave one night. He wasn't just a muscle boy- He was THE MUSCLE BOY- the biggest one in the scene at that time. His name was Eric and getting his attention was surprisingly easier than I thought considering all of the beautiful females that were around. He smiled and approached me immediately. He had seen me earlier- emerging from a bathroom stall with Bobby , a local body builder who wanted me to demonstrate my oral skills on his rather large appendage while he rolled. I was more than happy to oblige.

"Your boyfriend's hot," he said immediately.

"Your gay." I smiled as I said it.

"Disappointed?" He asked.

"Not at all," I replied. "But he's straight. Extremely well hung and he's not my boyfriend. Disappointed?"

"Sort of," he smiled. He was cute. Very cute. Not at all what you would expect of a gay male. Extremely masculine. Extremely beautiful body.

"Well, I just wanted to show you off anyway, not marry you." I said

"Sounds good. We'll show each other off. Actually, let me grab my friend Jason. You can show us both off."

Eric made his way around the bar and when he returned he produced another amazingly sculpted Adonis.

Jason was taller than Eric, very butch, cute, with a blonde flat top and a boyish innocence about him that I noticed immediately. He seemed most childlike when he smiled which was often. I loved him immediately and the feeling was mutual. I took them both by the hand and led them toward the dance floor. From her perch above the bar I saw Tish eyeing us. She smiled and gave me a thumbs up. Every eye was upon us as I danced between them. They ran they're hands all over me. The X carried us into the music. For a moment it seemed as if it were just the three of us. Touching, kissing, dancing. Tish told me later that everyone had been watching, hypnotized.

"What a picture," Tish had said.

"What bodies" Karen had said.

The three of us danced and rolled all night. For a moment, Eric focused his attention on Tish but after a few minutes of heavy petting, he grew tired of his little straight act and returned to me and Jason. When the rave was over, I followed the boys back to Eric's apartment.

It was an absolute mess. It was worse than that. It looked like a twister had blown through and carried the cleaning woman off to OZ.

"You live like pigs," I said.

"Shut and up and come here," Eric said as he peeled off his shirt and pants and jumped into bed. I climbed into bed beside him and Jason climbed in to. We layed there listening to music, winding down from the night. It felt incredible to be in the arms of these men. They were so strong and beautiful. It wasn't sexual. We just held each other, feeling the last residual effects of the X...then fell asleep as the sun began to come up.

CHAPTER 23

From that moment on, Jason, Eric and I were like scotch and soda. We did everything together. I pulled such a disappearing act on Lissette and the rest of the girls that they were pretty sure I was up to something big. We were in a different club every night of the week. We moved effortlessly through both gay and straight bars, causing a commotion wherever we went. People couldn't take their eyes off of me, them, us.

It was hypnotic. No one knew what to make of us. We danced together, played together, and people definitely had their own ideas about what else we were doing. We didn't care. I didn't know it then but I was building a legend...and my hot, young book ends were about to become one of the most enduring and lasting images of that legend. As the year progressed, there were more parties, more clubs, more raves and always the drugs.

Eric was developing a bad coke habit and was growing more and more distant. He began partying alone and before we knew what was happening he was out of control and in need of help. Jason and I did our best to help him but one day, he just shut both of us out completely.

One day after Eric had been particularly cruel to him, I found myself sitting in Jason's old mint condition Firebird. We were doing lines of coke off the dashboard and becoming increasingly wired. Jason was amazingly good looking. He was strong and extremely muscular. But he had a softness to his face, to his eyes. He had qualities that were so masculine and yet very childlike. He could be brash but it was rare. Most of the time he just seemed as though he were waiting for something spectacular to happen. Something better...almost like a child left too long at the fair. But on this day, he was sad and I could see it.

"Do you love him?" I asked.

"I don't know...I guess I love him," he replied.

"He doesn't want our help...and who are we to tell him to stop. Look at us."

"Yeah but we don't have a problem," he protested.

We were still very much in the early stages of addiction. Denial. The coke was making us antsy.

"Do you want to go out tonight?" he asked.

"Of course," I replied.

"Can I get ready at your house?" he asked. "I don't want to go all the way home."

Jason still lived at home with his parents on a sprawling ranch about an hour outside of Tampa. I thought about my step father. He hated strangers in the house. He would be very upset.

"Sure, why not!" I replied.

My mother loved Jason immediately. Mom was always a fan of the cute boys. Ricky, Eric...but Jason- he was special to her. Of course my stepfather pitched a fit about Jason but I basically told him to build a bridge and get over it. Jason seemed oblivious to my stepfather's tantrum and went about his business. That's what I loved about him. Jason loved me for me. He took me and everything that came with me including that ridiculous stepfather. He was a true friend in the purest sense. Many people thought we were a destructive influence on each other. But it truly was the beginning of a glorious friendship and a deep love and connection that I would feel for very few people in my life. That night, we started out at Howard Avenue Station, a gay club around the corner from my parent's house. Neither of us had a lot of money, so we decided to get drunk on beer and then hit it to an after hours that was going on later. I started chatting with a queen at the bar that I had known for years. She offered me a small blue pill.

"What does it do?" I asked.

"Makes you feel very slow motion," she replied in broken English.

I took the pill at about 3:30 am. Then I asked Jason if he wanted one. He declined. Thank God. We started out for the after hours. It was a big warehouse party being held near the airport. We were inside five minutes when I started to feel queasy. I clung to Jason.

"What's wrong?" He asked.

"I don't know," I replied. "I don't feel too good."

"I told you not to take that."

"I think I should eat something...I feel really weird."

Jason immediately steered me toward the door. Unlike most addicts who would have attempted to keep me at the party as long as possible, Jason's first priority was getting me to safety. That was the kind of person he was.

He put me in the car and drove me up the street to a Waffle House. Halfway through the breakfast, I passed out. I completely passed out with bacon in my mouth. The customers were not quite sure what to make of this beautiful, obviously fucked up couple.

"Should we call 911?" One of the waitresses asked.

"No, she's okay. She had too much to drink." He replied.

He hoisted me up and carried me in his arms out of the restaurant and into his car. That was all I remember and even that is just a blur. When I woke up the next morning, I was on a dirty bed in a cheap motel on a not so great side of east Hillsborough Ave. Jason was sitting in a chair by the bed, watching me intently.

"What happened?" I asked.

"I thought you overdosed," he replied. "Baby, you really scared me. I brought you here because I couldn't take you home. I've been up all night, giving you water and checking your breathing. . I'm sorry about the place but I only had twenty five dollars. It's all I could afford."

I looked up at him and smiled. I knew then and there that I had found a friend for life.

CHAPTER 24

My accidental overdose did nothing to deter my partying. I did however, in the name of good manners, steer clear of most small blue pills, at least for a little while. Jason and I continued our self destructive but oh so enjoyable ways. Over the next year, we became closer and closer. There was our whirlwind three day drug binge with Tish that carried us from Hammerjaxx to the very epicenter of a gay circuit party all in one weekend. For those of you unfamiliar, circuit parties are usually three to four day extravagances where the most beautiful fags -from all over the world -come together for three days of wild sex, drugs, dancing and oh yeah, charitable causes. This particular circuit party took place at—are you ready for this- Disney World. Yes, kiddies, it's true. For one weekend, every year, The Magic Kingdom becomes a hotbed of sexual depravity. If you didn't know- you better ask somebody. The three of us drove straight from Tampa on a wave of X and cocaine. We rolled all day. It's A Small World, Space Mountain, The Haunted Mansion. We did it all and kept on rolling. From there we followed the masses to Pleasure Island, an entertainment complex on the Disney compound and partied till the wee hours of the morning. Jason was a hit with the boys and Tish and I…well, we were on our way to taking complete leave of our senses. When a beautiful fag from South America offered me a bump of K- well, I took it. It didn't matter that I didn't even know what K was. I was hot, glamorous and in the middle of the hottest party on Earth. Who was I to refuse? Tish decided she would join me. We snorted the white powder from a clear glass bullet and waited for the high. We were bad, we were cool. Five minutes later we were in a box- literally in a box. We couldn't move- forward, backwards or sideways. We just sort of looked at each other, waiting for something else to happen, waiting for someone to tell us what the hell to do. Tish came out of it pretty quickly so she just sort of guided me around by my finger until I came to. I was a bit dazed.

"What the hell was that? Was that a high?"

"It must have been." Tish replied. She looked as confused as I was.

"That was fucking weird," I said.

Just then, the South American fag popped up.

"Hey Girls," he said, "Did you like it?"

Tish and I just looked at each other not quite sure what to say.

"Would you like another?" He asked.

I shrugged. "Sure," I replied.

...and that was our first gay circuit party.

***

After the circuit party, Tish, Jason and I began spending a lot of time together. Everyone else seemed to have temporarily deserted us. Lissette and Connie had become involved in-of all things- relationships. Sierra had dropped out of the scene for about a minute and Eric was back at his parents in New York trying to get his coke problem under control. So, the three of us just continued our all out assault on the central Florida rave scene. If there was a rave, we were there. Some of them went on for days and there we were- eating up the scene. Crazy thing was, no matter how many drugs we consumed or how many days we partied with no sleep, we were still the best looking people in the place. We just had it like that. DJ's and party promoters began to take notice of us and before we knew it, we were on every guest list and comp sheet in Florida. To make matters worse- or better—depending on your perspective, the dealers at the rave had taken notice of me too and I learned pretty quickly how to get what I wanted without having to pay for it. Hey, truth is, most of them were pretty cute and I would have sucked their dicks even if they hadn't hooked me up with ten hits of X. But that's me...just a friendly little cat!

CHAPTER 25

Well the day I dreaded had finally arrived. My unemployment ran out.

"You will find a job," my mother announced. "Playtime is over."

Reluctantly, I agreed. The one thing I always had going for me was my brain though there was no telling how long I could continue boasting if I continued down the road I was on. So I decided to take a little break. I found a job and took a few weeks off from Jason, The Rave, Tish, all of it. I began reading again which I had always loved. I fed my brain, took my vitamins, slept a lot, hung out with my mom and my nephew. It was nice. But by the second week, I was itching again. Tish was calling.

"Two Day Rave in Orlando called Hyperspace. It's on the Orlando State Fairgrounds. Are you game?"

"Let's go." I replied.

I poured my body into a skintight little silver dress and silver metallic combat boots. Tish chose something equally revealing and we set off in her Stealth. When we got there it looked like Woodstock. There was a traffic jam backed up for miles. People were abandoning their cars on the side of the road and walking. Shirtless muscle boys, raver chicks with backpacks and pig tails, and everyone who was anyone in the scene at that time. We found parking and hit it toward the entrance. Boys were spinning around. Tish and I had that affect on them, on everyone really. We dropped our pills and found our crew. All boys- Alfredo, Ralph and Trevor. Male strippers we knew from Tampa. Great friends, great accessories. Our pretty little picture was complete. I had a huge crush on Ralph and ended up clinging to him most of the night. Until, I saw Keith.

Keith was the most beautiful little banshee boy I had ever seen. Banshee boys were streety thug types- usually great dancers, incredible kissers and often very young. He was Puerto Rican and Italian with a tight, muscular body, liquid green eyes and the most perfect lips I had ever seen. He was wearing a backwards baseball cap, baggy jeans and a wife beater. He was dancing in the middle of a circle and everyone was cheering him on. His dancing- a mix of break, freestyle and just sexy fucking movement- was hypnotic. I decided then and there that I would have him. I mean if he moved like that on the floor, I could only imagine what else he was capable of...

I was hard to miss in my shiny silver mini and he danced his way toward me once he saw me watching him.

His movements were cocky and self assured. The little bastard knew he was fine.

"What's up?" he asked.

"What's your name?" I asked.

"Keith. I met you at Hammerjaxx, remember?" His tone was as cocky as the smirk on his face.

"Vaguely," I lied.

"Yeah, my cousin told me you were a man. I thought that was pretty fucked up. You know, the way you fooled me."

"Did I fool you?" I asked innocently. "Maybe your perception was just a little off."

I turned around to walk away. Fuck him, I thought. I don't need his ass.

"Do you want to dance?" He called after me.

I smiled to myself. Then I spun around and looked him straight in the eye.

"Why the fuck should I dance with you now?" I asked.

He gave me that cocky smile and took my hand.

"Because you want to," He replied.

We walked toward the floor and I suddenly felt very warm inside.

"How old are you?" I asked.

"Seventeen," he replied, "But don't worry, I'll fuck you better than any man you've ever been with."

And if memory serves me correctly, and believe me it does, he did!! You just don't forget someone like that.

CHAPTER 26

So what do you do with a boy that fucks you like you've never been fucked before? Move in with him, of course. I was working. He borrowed money from his dad. His parents gave their consent and we were off to the races. We found a small apt near USF. I was actually dropping him off at high school in the morning before I left for work. It was the quickest living arrangement of my young life. It lasted exactly one month. The relationship lasted a little longer. A little more than a year. I thought I loved him. I guess I did. There were moments of true intimacy. He had done and seen so much in his young life that he wasn't really seventeen at all. But he still had a lot to learn and I wasn't going to be the one to teach him. Over the year we tried to maintain our relationship as he moved from Tampa to New York to Massachusetts. After a failed reconciliation at his father's home on Cape Cod, we called it quits for good and moved on.

The problem with having a boyfriend when your friends don't is that you tend to alienate them without even meaning to. Tish and Jason had been hanging out with out me and trying to track them down was no easy feat.

They had taken to hanging out with the Orlando ate-up's. Ate-up was a term that people in the know used to refer to those in the scene whose brains and sense of fashion had been compromised by the use of too many pharmaceutical libations. In the most extreme cases, some ate-up's could be akin to the Florida cockroach. It's not a cute scene. However, it only made sense that they would be going out in Orlando. The drugs were better there. I had to find them. In the meantime, I gave Hector a call. It had been awhile since we'd hung out. He had helped me sneak Keith into a couple of the clubs while we were together and though our friendship tended to have it's questionable moments, we were still quite capable of going out and having fun together.

"I think I'm doing Ybor but you can come if you want," He said.

"Can we get some coke?" I asked.

"Yeah, let me call a friend. Pick me up in one hour." he replied.

I slid into a skintight little black dress, slicked my hair back and set off. Hector was waiting outside his place when I pulled up. He jumped in.

"Hey Girl," he said with a kiss.

"Hey Girl," I replied.

"Did you get the coke?" I asked.

"Head toward the river," he instructed, "We're going by my friend Andrew's."

"Andrew. Do I know Andrew?"

"No," he replied, "But you will."

CHAPTER 27

So what's the last thing you throw at a beautiful coke head with a lot of time on her hands and a Scarface complex? Why, the biggest drug dealer in town of course. My first meeting with Andrew Marcello was a brief but memorable one. He was standing outside of my future residence when we pulled up. He was handsome but not in a conventional way. He was short but he had strong Italian features, beautiful eyes and an amazing charisma. He was older but definitely not old. Andrew leaned into the passenger window and threw the coke on Hectors lap.

"What's up Hector?" He asked. He seemed very genuine and friendly.

"Andrew, this is my friend Sophia." Hector was smiling. He knew what was about to happen. Hector had a way of putting unsuspecting people together in rather unusual circumstances, sometimes for his enjoyment but mostly to see what would happen.

"Sophia…." Andrew smiled as he repeated my name. The look on his face was love at first sight but it vanished quickly.

"Isn't she beautiful?" Hector asked innocently.

"Very," Andrew replied.

"Well, we better run along," Hector said after a moment of watching us make eye contact. "Don't want to be late for 1509."

Andrew kissed my hand and as I drove away, I knew that this was the beginning of something big and by the satisfied look on Hectors face, so did he.

***

"Andrew wants to see you again," Hector said when he spoke to me a few days later.

"What?" I asked.

"Andrew wants to see you again," he repeated.

"Hector, he's not really my type…Does he even know about me?" I asked.

"I told him but I don't know if he really gets it or even cares. Look, his daughter Michelle is one of my best friends and she is in town from Miami. She's having a party at Masquerade tonight. Andrew will be there. Just come by and see what happens."

Hector could be quite persuasive when he wanted to be.

"All right, I'll meet you at Masquerade at midnight." I said.

For the party, I chose a sexy long sleeved black mini dress and black patent leather boots up to the knee. My hair was wild and curly. It was one of those nights where everything came together. Truthfully, I have lots of those nights but even by today's standards, I looked pretty fucking hot. Michelle's party was getting more and more packed when I arrived. She recognized me and waved me the past the line that had begun to form outside of the club. As I approached her, I couldn't help but admire her. Michelle was beautiful. She was blonde and had a body to die for. She was considered the top bikini model in Tampa and had won several competitions and thousands of dollars in cash and prizes before calling it quits and moving to Miami. She had even won a corvette once. She was definitely a legend in Tampa.

"Hey girl," she said warmly embracing me. "Hector's inside with my dad."

I stepped into the club and was immediately excited. The music was great and there was a sense of promise in the air. I found Hector and Andrew having drinks by the bar.

"Hi Guys," I said sweetly.

"Hey Girl," Hector said dramatically. "I don't think anyone is coming. There is no one here."

"Well, I'm here, you're here, Andrew's here…someone is definitely here." I replied.

He laughed and walked toward the front of the club leaving me alone with Andrew.

Andrew smiled nervously. "Hey Sophia," he said.

I smiled and thought about what I could say to put him at ease. He seemed sweet even a bit shy.

"Do I make you nervous Andrew?" I asked.

"No," he replied, "Why would you make me nervous?"

"Have a drink with me," I said ignoring the question.

"What do you drink?" He asked.

"Tequila. Cuervo straight up." I replied.

The look on his face was classic.

"You take tequila straight?" He asked.

"Tequila straight," I replied.

That night, I got to know Mr. Andrew Marcello a little better. Over shots of tequila, we discussed our lives. We discussed his two failed marriages and what he thought went wrong. His recent legal troubles were weighing on him and he was honest about them. We discussed my issues and my dreams for the future and we discussed my past. All the while, he listened. Like an old friend. Like an old, trusted friend. I felt safe with Andrew, almost from the beginning. When I left the club that night, we had made plans for the following Wednesday evening.

"I want to make you dinner," he said.

"I'd like that," I replied.

And just like that- It was a date.

CHAPTER 28

Our first date was magnificent. Andrew was an incredible cook. He prepared fettuccini from scratch while I sipped a very nice cabernet. His home was beautiful. The music was right. We laughed and talked.

I didn't have to try to be sexy nor did I feel the need to impress him. The conversation and rapport just flowed, naturally. He was happy to see that I did indeed have an appetite.

"You are so tiny, but look how you eat." He said with a smile.

I stopped suddenly, not sure of myself.

"Don't stop," he laughed. "I love it. You are enjoying the meal. I like that."

We both smiled and the evening continued. More wine, more conversation, more laughter. There was a moment of silence between us when I suddenly felt him take my hand in his. He looked at me, truly looked at me as though he could see beneath the make-up and the hair...He looked at me as though he knew the scared little boy inside. More importantly, he looked at me as though none of it mattered.

"I think you are very beautiful," he said.

The way he said it changed everything. It wasn't just a comment. It wasn't just a compliment. It was profound.

"I want to tell you something," he continued. "I have never looked at someone like you and thought, I could be with this person. I'm a straight man from the old school. I'm not gay. But you're a woman to me. From the moment I saw you...you're a woman to me. I deal drugs for a living but that's not who I am. I'm a good person who made some bad choices. But I love my kids and my friends and I take care of the people who matter to me. I want to be your friend."

I stared at him as he spoke. I knew he spoke from his heart. He would never lie to me or intentionally try to hurt me. I believed this man was unlike anyone I had ever met. How right, I would turn out to be. Looking back, I know that what he ultimately fulfilled in me was the burning need for a father figure in my life. It was a need I had always had. It was dream that had never been realized. But at that young age, I thought I was falling in love. And maybe in some way, I did.

CHAPTER 29

Life with Andrew was surprisingly easy and carefree. Over the next few months we became closer and closer. I began spending more and more time at his place. We did movies, dinner. If I wanted to go out with my friends, I did. If I wanted coke, I asked for it. He never told me no and he never asked for a penny. His coke was the best. I would score an 8 ball and hit the clubs with whoever was available- Sierra, Hector, Lissette, Connie. It didn't matter. I just wanted someone to party with. Andrew didn't really do coke which is probably why he was so successful as a dealer. He didn't like me doing it either. But I think he knew that if he tried to control me, I would run. So, he let me do my thing in the hopes that I would tire of it. It took about three months of hardcore out-every-night partying for me to get the message. One morning, after an especially brutal night of self destruction, I had my first nose bleed. He found me in the downstairs bathroom with a towel in my hand.

"You got to slow down," Andrew said. "You are going to burn a hole in your nose if you haven't already."

"I will," I promised. But of course, I didn't. I continued. Then one day, he gave me an ultimatum.

"Look Sophia, this has got to stop. Either I'm your friend and we share our lives together- or I'm your supplier and you start paying and we go our separate ways. I care too much to watch you destroy yourself. Don't you want to take a break for awhile? I think we have a good thing. I would like to see where it leads. But I will not go on with you like this."

So I stopped. Just like that. I didn't touch cocaine for two months. I got a job, cleaned up my act and decided to concentrate on Andrew and I. After all, our relationship was the best thing I had going for me. My mother loved him. Even my stepfather liked him. He may have been a drug dealer but he was also a damn good man- even I could see that. So at twenty three years old, I decided to set up house with a man 25 years older than myself. I knew all the stories and so did he. Despite pressure from his daughter, his friends and anyone else who thought they had a say in his life, Andrew happily helped me move my clothes and the rest of my personal possessions into his house on a warm summer day. It was the beginning of beautiful, chaotic bliss.

***

My relationship with Andrew had its wonderful moments. It had some pretty bad ones too. But that first year was great. Being together was a learning process for both of us. Sexually, he had some issues to deal with. I had to curb my partying in order to accommodate my new arrangement. But we were both determined to prove everyone wrong and make it work. If I got restless, he had no problem with me going out as long as I promised to be back at a decent hour. Sometimes, I was. Sometimes, I wasn't. That was just me. He understood but he didn't like it. As the months went on and my little fling stretched into a year long relationship, I became more and more restless. I lived in a beautiful home, Andrew gave me everything I wanted and still something was missing. I began going out more which put a huge strain on our relationship. He became insecure and accused me of cheating. He stopped giving me drugs and I retaliated by spending more and more nights away, partying in clubs with people who never told me no. Eventually, the beautiful dreams we built together began to shatter.

One morning, high on cocaine and X, I began throwing my clothes into my car. When he came home, I was almost completely packed.

"Where are you going?" He asked.

"I'm leaving you. I cant take this anymore." I replied.

"Take what, Sophia?" He asked. "All I've ever done is love you, protect you. You wanted a home, I gave you one. You wanted money, I gave you money. You wanted drugs, I gave you drugs. What is it that you cant take anymore of? The last time I checked, everything you took was all that you asked for."

The look on his face was devastating. I had hurt this person. He looked hurt.

"Please don't go," He said it simply as though it meant nothing.

I climbed in my car and drove away. I could feel the tears welling up in my eyes. I had no where to go. I had no money. But at that moment, I felt as though it was the right thing to do, the only thing to do. It may have been the drugs, but something inside told me it was time.

CHAPTER 30

Of course, I went home. The first thing I did was call Jason. We went out that night and got fucked up for two days. By the time I got home, my mother had had it.

"You better figure something out and quick. I will not have you using this house as a hotel room. I understand that you felt the need to leave Andrew. I don't know why. It's not my business. But I know what you are doing and I don't like it. So get it together or you will have to find somewhere else to live."

I listened but didn't say anything. I knew she was right. My mother would always take me back. But how many times was I going to run home with my tail between my legs? When was I finally going to stand on my own two feet? I decided that something had to give. I sat down and thought about my life. I had been partying for quite awhile now. I was basically getting nowhere. I was seriously in danger of becoming a complete and total fuck up with absolutely no redeeming qualities. I was in my prime. If I was going to grab life by the balls, it had to be now. I knew that I would never go back to office work or a structured work environment of any kind, for that matter. I loved the idea of stripping. So many of my girlfriends did it and they made it seem so glamorous. At the time, Tish was bi-coastal. She was traveling to Vegas, had apartments in both Tampa and Myrtle Beach and was earning upwards of $1,000.00 a day. I approached her for advice.

"Come with me to Myrtle Beach," she said. "I can get you a gig at Illusions as a cage dancer. It's not the best but at least you'll be out of Tampa and making some money. You should start saving for your implants. Once you get your breasts done, it's easy street. Trust me. Then you can dance topless. No one has to know that your a ts. Just hit the upscale topless clubs and watch the dough roll in."

I took her advice and later that week was following her, with Lissette (fresh from her sex change surgery) in tow, to Myrtle Beach. Getting work at Illusions was a cake walk. It was the largest gay techno club in Myrtle Beach. Tish's boyfriend Moz was a stripper there. They hired me immediately. I climbed into a cage suspended above the dance floor wearing a neon green bikini and white go-go boots. At the end of the night, I had a whole new set of fans and only thirty four one dollar bills. I was not a happy camper.

"Try the bikini bars," Tish suggested. "They're a little ghetto but you'll make money. Just be careful and watch your back."

Next stop was Bottoms Up, a not so upscale bikini bar where some very out of shape and over age would be dancers were shaking their money makers to the strains of Skynard and Springsteen. I was unamused but not half as unamused as they were when I took the stage and the customers started lining up to throw money at me. I am not exaggerating. The men literally formed a line around the stage and began throwing money at me. Every other dancer in the place ceased to exist. I smiled and went with it. On stage I mimicked the dancers I had always loved and admired- Sierra, Tish. I felt alive and powerful and I wasn't even high. When I finished my set, I stepped off stage and began working the crowd. The men were on me so quick I barely had a chance to breathe.

Every one of them wanted a private dance.

The burly security guard outside the private rooms gave me a quick once over and told me the rules.

"Nothing crazy. No friction, no real contact. Keep it clean. Dances are ten dollars and I get half."

I smiled sweetly and took my first customer by the hand. When I got him in the room, I laid down my own rules.

"The dance is twenty five dollars." I said firmly.

The guy looked at me in surprise.

"The guy outside just told me it was ten."

"No, he told ME it was ten, and I'm telling you, it's twenty five."

"The other girls charge ten."

"Then have one of them dance for you. I have a line of guys outside waiting so make up your mind."

The guy pulled out a wad of cash and began counting out the money.

"I hope you are worth it," he said rudely.

"Oh, I'm worth a helluva a lot more than that but I'll be sure to give you what you pay for," I replied.

So I danced. I moved in ways that allowed him to feel my ass, my back but never my breasts or my crotch. While dancing, I moaned softly. When I faced him, I looked him straight in the eyes. Sliding down on my knees, I buried my face inches from his crotch then threw my hair back and before I knew it, I had given my first lap dance. The music was over and I was ready for the next guy. I didn't even make it out the door. The security guard stopped me.

"Might as well stay inside. You got a whole line out here and these bitches are pissed."

"They'll be alright," I said. "Send me the next one."

I gave several lap dances in that little room that night. With every one, I became more and more confident and more cocky. Within an hour, I had made several hundred dollars. I decided it was time to bail before someone found out my business. I gave security his cut and headed toward the manager to arrange my pay out. I made it five steps when I realized I was in somewhat of a situation. A tired blonde with a little too much ass stepped out in front of me and blocked my way. The small brunette with her was even more unattractive.

The conversation went something like this:

Blonde: Bitch, I think you stole my money.

Me: I didn't steal shit from you. I've been dancing for an hour straight and that security guard has been watching me the whole time. You've got the wrong girl.

Blonde: I don't think so. You need to hand over your shit because were going to count this and get this settled now.

Me: Bitch, you have definitely got the wrong girl now. I aint handin'over a goddamn thing. I suggest you get the fuck out of my way before I lay your fat ass out. You aren't dealing with one of these little girls in here. You better know what you are doing.

Well that's all it took. We went at it. The crowd swarmed us as we began flaying away at each other. The security guard tried to separate us and I decked him too. In the end, she was topless on the floor and I was being carried out of the club by the manager and the DJ. As it turned out, the fight was the best thing that could have happened. I kept every dime I had made, didn't have to pay the house and I learned a very valuable lesson. I will always be better, smarter, prettier than the average stripper so a career in stripping would always give me problems. Coincidentally, I ran in to the bouncer later that night at an after hours club and we had an amazing morning. From what I can remember.

CHAPTER 31

"Please come home." The voice on the other end of the line was gentle and kind with just a hint of sadness. It was Andrew.

"I'm not coming home." I said simply.

"Your mom told me about the dancing. She's worried about you. But she says that you wont come home until you have the money for your implants."

"That's right."

"How much do you need?" he asked.

"Four thousand dollars," I replied.

"If I give you the money will you come home?"

I was silent for a moment and thought carefully before I answered.

"I will come back to Tampa but I will not come back to you."

"Just get in the car and go back to your parent's house. When you get there, your mom will have the money you need."

"Why are you doing this?" I asked.

"Because I love you and because I love your mom and she's worried about you."

I hung up the phone and told Lissette that we were going back to Tampa.

"I think I'm going to stay," she said. "I'm making money at The Crazy Horse so I might as well work it for all it's worth."

"Suit yourself," I said.

The next day, I climbed back into my car and raced back to Tampa. When I got home, my mom threw her arms around me. I felt so safe when she embraced me. She had a big smile on her face and seemed really happy that I was home.

"I made stuffed green pepper," she said.

It was my favorite dish.

"Thanks mom. I missed you."

"I missed you too."

For the first time I noticed that something was different about my mom. I knew she hadn't been feeling well. For the first time, she didn't look well either.

"Mom, are you okay?" I asked.

"Sure, I feel okay." She quickly changed the subject.

"Nick gave me the money."

"Good, he said he would." I replied.

My mom took me by the hand and I could see just a hint of tears. Then she spoke softly and with more feeling than I could have ever hoped for.

"Honey, I love you. No matter what. You have always been my baby. My sweet little boy. I may not always agree with the things you do but I want you to be happy. If I had the money to help you with your surgeries, I would. But you know I cant. Not now. But I want you to be happy...for the rest of your life."

Then she embraced me warmly. Two weeks later, my mom took me to get my breasts done. I was out of commission for three weeks. She didn't leave my side for a minute.

CHAPTER 32

The ad that changed my life was in the back of a Nightmoves magazine and said exactly this:

BEAUTIFUL PRE-OP TRANSSEXAULS WANTED FOR MOD-ELING AND ESCORT WORK. UPSCALE SERVICE PROVIDES CLI-ENT REFERELS. $1000.00 A WEEK MIN. NO EXPERIENCE NEED-ED. BREAST IMPLANTS A PLUS.

The ad gave a FT. Lauderdale phone number. I didn't even hes-itate. I called the number and got an answering service. I left my name and number and hoped for the best. A few hours later, the call was returned. It was considerably easier than I thought to sell myself to the voice on the other end of the line. Three days later I was in Lauderdale. The man that met me at the airport was slight of build and easily intimidated. Today, I don't even recall his name. He was insignificant to me almost immediately because he was unable to make good on his promises. He simply didn't have the contacts. I was almost ready to head home when he introduced me to James. I met James on my second night in town. James was an "agent" of some renown. He worked mostly with females but was looking for a beautiful transsexual to jump start a "house" he was hoping to create in Boston. James was nice enough. He offered respect and trust and asked for the same in return. I gave him a chance. He delivered. I n exchange for forty percent of my fee, I used his house and his con-tacts. I made quite a bit with him and for him, first in Lauderdale and later in Boston. We worked together for several months and he taught me a lot about the business, for better or worse. Ironically, it was one of James' clients that would lead me astray and into the clutches of a much more charismatic and sinister "agent". His name was Riley. I saw him only once. The call was pretty quick. He seemed nice enough but didn't say much. As he was leaving, he surveyed my surroundings. He gave me five hundred dollars and handed me a card. The card was sleek and black and had only a name and phone number.

"Give this guy a call," he said, He's a first class manager. Don't waste your beauty in this place."

I never saw Riley again. But two days later when I returned to Tampa, I called the number he had given me and left a message for Anthony Lavelle, the man whose name appeared on the card. Ironically, it was another Ft. Lauderdale number. Who knew south Florida was such a hotbed of prostitution? A few hours later, my mom told me I had a phone call. I rushed to answer.

"Hello."

A strong masculine voice on the other end of the line came across clearly.

"Is this Sophia?" He asked.

"Yes."

"Hello Sophia. I'm Anthony Lavelle. I own a service in South Florida that caters to gentlemen with tastes of a different persuasion. I understand that you might be interested in working for me."

"I may be interested in working with you, not for you." I replied.

"Fair enough," he said. "Tell me a little about yourself."

"I'm exactly what you're looking for. Why don't you tell me about yourself and how much money we can make." I replied.

"You're pretty confident Sophia. Can you back up that attitude with beauty and intelligence or are you just- as we in the industry like to call it- a one trick pony?"

"I guess you'll have to find out." I replied.

After a long silence, he spoke.

"Riley told me about you. He says you're very beautiful. But if your going to work for me you need to forget about what you think you know. You need to forget that place he found you. My clients will never know about that house in Boston. Understood?"

"I understand." I replied.

"When can you be back in Lauderdale?"

"I don't know anything about you or your service," I replied. "I'm not just going to take a four hour drive because you ask me too."

"I didn't ask you to drive. I will arrange for a first class ticket- round trip- if you are what I'm looking for, we'll work something out. If not, well you can always go back to Tampa."

I was silent as I pondered the situation. I knew nothing of this man. I barely knew myself or if I was even capable of doing the things required of this so called job. He must have sensed my hesitation.

"Sophia, he said, "Trust me. It's all legit. You will be safe."

The next morning, against my mother's better judgment, I boarded a plane for Lauderdale. Of course, I hadn't told her the extent of my plans- only that I was going to see a friend I knew in South Florida. Looking back, I realize how dangerous my actions could have been. Anthony Lavelle could have been a maniac, a murderer, or both. I was two days shy of my twenty second birthday when I boarded that plane. It was the best thing I could have ever done and the worst mistake of my life.

CHAPTER 33

My premonition that Anthony Lavelle could have been a maniac or a murderer was completely off base. He was worse. He was a serial seducer of desperate young girls. He was a pimp disguised as a businessman. He lived in a mansion on Harbor Beach, drove a Ferrari and had a masters degree in business. There wasn't a flashy thing about him. He was very refined, even elegant. Articulate. Intelligent. Caring. A Monster. What I was too young to realize was that all the pomp and ceremony of his surroundings didn't change what he was or what he did. I thought hookers were girls in hot pants that hung out downtown and stuck needles in their arms. Hookers weren't beautiful, savvy business women with platinum cards and a Mercedes in the driveway. That's where he got me. He changed my perception without even trying. Two days in that house surrounded by beautiful women- all of whom seemed happy and carefree- and I was hooked.

"You are what I've been looking for," he told me. "I have beautiful women. You can find them everywhere. But a beautiful transsexual is the future of this business. You are that girl. You are not just beautiful, your classy and your smart...and your hungry. You want to work. I'm going to have Jade take you shopping at Bal Harbor. Nothing but the best. I want you to stay here for about a week. Let the girls show you the ropes and then if you are ready, I already have a client lined up in Boston."

"Boston?" I began to protest.

"He'll pay you five thousand for two days and take you shopping."

"And what do you get out of this?" I asked

"I already arranged a payout for myself with the client. You personally kick back $500.00 of your money and keep the rest."

"What about the clothes today?" I asked.

"A write-off. I don't expect it back."

I looked at Anthony and my gut told me to trust him. I had no choice but to trust my gut. He walked me toward the front door where Jade was waiting with the Ferrari. He handed me an American Express platinum card and kissed me on the cheek.

"Buy whatever you want," He said.

As I was getting in the car, he called after me.

"By the way, you can stay here as long as you like or at the apt in Boston. All I ask is that your ready to work if called upon."

"Thanks," I said, "But if I make the kind of money your promising, I should be able to afford my own place."

He smiled. I climbed into the Ferrari beside one of the most beautiful blondes I had ever seen and roared off.

***

Jade and I became fast friends. I figured I had better since she was the one in charge of showing me the ropes.

She was beautiful. She was tall and lithe with beautiful lips and perfect skin. She had an air of confidence about her that bordered on arrogance but I liked her immediately. She was always impeccably dressed and stressed the importance of arriving on time and dressed to kill. We spent thousands of dollars on clothes that day. By the time our shopping trip was over, I had everything a high class call girl could need. Exhausted by shopping, Jade suggested lunch and a martini at The Clevelander. As we waited for our drink, Jade began schooling me on the tricks of the trade.

"Rule Number One- Don't fall in love. You are going to meet a lot of very attractive men. Some of them are wealthy. Most of them are wealthy beyond any stretch of the imagination. They will shower you with gifts and treat you like a princess. But never forget- most of them are married and you're the fantasy. They only want one thing from you no matter what they say. They will never give up half of what they own to run off with you or me or the both of us."

"Rule Number Two: Never lose sight of the objective. Money is priority one. Never settle for what the agency gets you. If Anthony arranges for five thousand, charge seven. Never spend your own money while working not even to tip the bathroom attendant. If he offers you anything of any monetary value, take it. If it's a piece of jewelry that you hate, don't hold off for something you like. It may not come. Take it, pawn it and buy what you like. If he asks you to wear it on the next date, act upset and say it was stolen by one of the other girls. He'll buy you a new one. Most women don't want to be call girls. Always remember what brought you to this point and you'll never lose sight of the objective."

"Rule Number Three: Always look better than your best. Make it a point to out do every woman in the room including the girls you may have to work with including me. Nails, hair, toes should be done weekly. Never wear the same dress with the same client. Eat a little but not a lot when having dinner. ALWAYS insist upon the best champagne, the best restaurants and a limo so that it weeds out the guys who don't want to spend as much."

"Rule Number Four: Always listen. Talk but more importantly, listen. These guys need someone to talk to. If they just landed a huge deal, act excited and celebrate with them. If they're going through a painful divorce, be sympathetic and order only one glass of wine. If the guy just wants to fuck you and dinner seems to be something he really isn't in to- order appetizers and dessert. Make him wait and keep him wanting you all the more."

"Rule Number Five: Fuck his brains out and never lose sight of the objective."

I studied Jade. The name suited her. She had a detachment about her that seemed so cool, so...jaded. I watched as she discreetly pulled a small bag of cocaine from her purse and did a bump from her perfectly manicured nail right there at the table. I figured she must have been doing this a long time.

"How old are you?" I asked.

"Eighteen," She replied.

CHAPTER 34

So that is how it all started. Jade showed me the ropes. Anthony arranged a few "test runs" with willing regular clients who paid me $500.00 for dinner and thirty minutes of private time afterward. He let the clients know ahead of time that I was a transsexual so that there would be no surprises later. They were to "rate" my table manners, my personality, my skills as an effective and articulate communicator and my ability to give head. Believe it or not, these "test runs" would be my final initiation in to the world of sex for sale. The men were all attractive. Most were professionals though one was a trust fund baby. It was easier than I thought or so I thought. The game is an easy one to play in the beginning. It changes as you go.

I still remember the day that Anthony told me I was ready to leave for Boston. It was a Friday. I was sitting by the pool with Casey, a beautiful porn star from LA who was staying at the house for a couple of days. I was talking to my mom on the phone and she seemed worried but I was assuring her that everything was okay and that I would be home within a week.

"I need you in Boston for a couple of days." He said.

"When?" I asked.

"Tomorrow. Two days with one of our very best clients. He's the reason you're here Sophia. He's tired of the same old thing. He wants something a little different. He requested a girl like you. You do this right and you and I could make a lot of money."

"Fine. I know I'm ready for this." I was confident I could handle it. How bad could it be?

"Great. Jade has arranged for your ticket. You will have your own suite in the hotel. Don't fall asleep with him or agree to spend the night in his room. Once you're evening and private time is over, go back to your room. Meet him again in the morning for breakfast and shopping and go about your day. Business as usual. You come back Monday morning. He'll give you the money when you arrive. Put it in the hotel safe and don't spend a dime of your own money. He's a gentlemen. He has been with several of the girls and is what we like to refer to as a preferred client. Please handle yourself accordingly."

"I will." I promised.

Later that night as Jade helped me pack, I asked her about something.

"Should I change my name?"

"I thought you had," she replied.

"No, I mean, should I use another name while working other than my real name?"

"Of course, the less they know about you the better."

"What do you think?"

She looked at me. Her eyes looked as though they had lived a thousand lives.

"Raquel." she said finally.

I thought about it and loved it immediately.

"Why Raquel?" I asked.

She continued folding my clothes without looking up.

"Because you remind me of a girl I knew when she first started. Raquel was her real name."

"What happened to her?" I asked.

"Who knows," she replied sadly.

***

The next morning, Jade drove me to the airport. As I was getting out of the car, she grabbed my hand.

"He's basically a nice guy with some very sick fetishes. He won't try to hurt you and he's perfectly normal outside of the bedroom. Just remember, you make the rules, you call the shots. Don't do anything you don't want to do. The good thing about Anthony is that he's not your run of the mill pimp. He'll back you up whatever your limits.

He's smart enough to know that a healthy, happy girl keeps the money rolling in."

"Thanks Jade."

I gave her a hug and I'll never forget the look on her face as I got out of that car. How tired that beautiful eighteen year old face seemed, how desperate. It was the last time I would see her alive.

CHAPTER 35

For all practical purposes, I have changed many of the names of the people whose stories appear on these pages. The reason for the anonymity is because not only are some of these people known to millions of fans throughout the world but more importantly, they are fathers and husbands and I do not believe in disgracing innocent women and children. My first client and ultimately the man responsible for taking me to depths of depravity that I never knew existed was an enormously wealthy and very influential investment banker with offices in New York, Zurich and Geneva. He had it all. Political clout, famous friends and enough money and power to buy anything and anyone he wanted. And if all that failed...he had the drugs. Lots of drugs. We'll call him David. David saw one girl a month and arranged for her to join him wherever in the world he happened to be at the time. For three and half weeks of every month, David was a loving father, a non existent husband and a brilliant businessman. But it was that one weekend of every month that he truly came alive. He turned off the cell phone and gave in to unbridled and unadulterated lust.

When I arrived in Boston, I found myself growing more and more excited. This is just like a movie I told myself. I felt like one of those glamorous jet-setting heroines in a Jackie Collins novel. I was wearing a black Gucci skirt, a white button down shirt and strappy Via Spiga high heeled sandals. My hair was slicked back and I was wearing a huge pair of Chanel sunglasses. Every man in first class had attempted an introduction but I had remained aloof and unapproachable. I tried to remember what Jade had told me. Be nice but unavailable, never too friendly with strangers on a plane.

As I left the plane and entered the terminal, I saw a chauffeur holding a sign with my name on it. I introduced myself and he led me downstairs to baggage claim. After collecting my suitcase, he led me outside to a sleek new Mercedes and opened the door for me. There was champagne on ice and a note which read:

WILL MEET YOU IN THE HOTEL BAR AFTER YOU SETTLE IN. PLEASE DON'T KEEP ME WAITING TOO LONG. WEAR THE DRESS THAT'S ON YOUR BED. IN THE HOTEL ROOM SAFE, YOU'LL FIND THE MONEY AND A LITTLE SOMETHING TO GET YOU STARTED. THE CODE TO OPEN THE SAFE IS 5984. Xo, D

I enjoyed the ride from Logan airport. It felt great to be back in Boston. Even today it remains one of my favorite cities in the world. I was staying at a first class hotel in the heart of downtown. My suite was spectacular with sweeping views of the park. There was a beautiful red wrap dress on the bed. It was sexy but elegant. It was a daytime dress but could easily be used at night with the right accessories. I never liked myself in red but David loved red and as I would soon learn, what David wanted David got. After changing and freshening up, I went to the safe. I punched in the code and there it was- $5000.00 dollars in fresh crisp one hundred dollar bills. There was also a small jewel encrusted pillbox. I couldn't tell if the jewels were real or not. Didn't matter. What was inside was more enticing. Just enough cocaine to get me going. I cut out two fat lines on the bathroom counter, rolled up one of the hundreds and snorted them quickly. It had to be some of the best shit I'd ever had. I looked at myself in the mirror. I looked amazing. I felt amazing. It was time to do this and do it right. Do it better than any other girl he'd ever seen. It was show time.

CHAPTER 36

When I entered the hotel lobby, I turned every head in the place. I had no idea what my guy looked like, so I just made my way to the bar and waited. I did look amazing and every man in the room couldn't keep his eyes off of me.

"Hello beautiful," a voice behind me whispered.

I turned and found myself face to face with one of the most distinguished men I had ever seen. He was tall and his body seemed perfect for the expensive tailor made suit he was wearing. His face was thin and handsome with high cheekbones and dark eyes. His hair was short and he was clean shaven with just a hint of shadow. He spoke with a European accent but I couldn't place it. I figured him to be about forty but he could have been older.

"I am David." He introduced himself and kissed me lightly on the cheek.

I made a point of looking him straight in the eyes when I introduced myself. I found him attractive immediately. There has always been something about an impeccably dressed, well preserved older man.

"Anthony didn't exaggerate when he said you were something special. I watched you turn every head when you walked in the room. You have a lot of confidence, especially for a girl that…well, a woman of your nature."

I leaned forward and squeezed his hand as I spoke.

"Confidence comes from within, David. As I'm sure you know it has nothing to do with having a penis. The fact that I do happen to have one, makes me all the more sure of that…and of myself."

He smiled, clearly pleased with my reply.

"Intelligent too. Shall we?" He held out his hand.

I took it like a lady as he escorted me through the bar to the restaurant. Over dinner- and two very expensive bottles of wine- we talked. David did most of the talking but revealed very little about himself. He seemed more interested in me. I answered his questions politely but volunteered no information. I was coy and sexy but not cheap. I teased him but playfully. When he reached across the table to touch my arm or my hand or stroke my cheek, I didn't withdraw but drew toward him as though it were a touch I had longed for all of my life. My ability to play a part had always been a part of me. I should have been an actress but I guess fate had other plans for me. When he signaled for the check, I assumed we would go back to his room together but David had something else in mind.

"Raquel, do you see that very handsome young man at the bar?" He pointed to a very hot guy in a tight black sweater and soft leather pants. He was beyond good looking. The guy raised his beer bottle in our direction.

"Yes, I do."

"I hired him. For you. He is one of the most famous adult film stars in the world. To get him here tonight, I had to spring for that Gucci ensemble he's wearing and promise him half an ounce of co-caine. That's it. That's all he wanted."

I was silent, just as Jade had told me to be. He continued speaking.

"Now, I realize that this wasn't part of the deal and something tells me that your not the type of girl who likes a surprise without proper compensation...The dress you have on cost me $2000.00 You keep the dress and the money I've already paid you and fuck that hot young stud while I watch and we'll call it even...Sound good?"

I smiled. I paused before answering. My reply had to be dramatic and perfectly timed.

"No, I don't think so."

He seemed surprised.

"Excuse me?"

"I said, I don't think so. That wasn't the deal."

He was silent as he studied me. I said nothing but kept staring him straight in the eye.

"He's very handsome Raquel and I assure you quite well endowed. I hear girls like you enjoy a big cock."

I could see the attitude was shifting. The gentleman was quickly giving way to the deviant.

"That's not the point," I responded firmly.

"What is the point, Raquel?"

"The point is that we had an agreement that did not include your handsome young friend over there. I will gladly get into bed with him because let's face it- who wouldn't- but I need to be compensated additionally."

He laughed aloud.

"Compensated for fucking a man that you would fuck for free under any other circumstances?"

"That's right."

His cold eyes stared me down for a solid minute before they turned bright again. Just like that -back to a perfect gentleman.

"How much?" He asked.

"A thousand dollars...and no anal." I replied.

"Done."

He paid the check and I followed him over to meet the man I would be acting out his fantasy with.

"Raquel, this is Bo."

Bo was even more gorgeous up close. I couldn't wait to get my hands on him.

"I'm going to give you guys a few moments to get acquainted," David said. "Discuss what a freak I am and all that good stuff and I will meet you upstairs in 15 minutes. Be naked when I get there."

Bo and I walked like obedient hookers toward the elevators. He took me by the small of my back. His hands were strong and when he spoke, his tone was sexy and masculine.

"Don't worry baby. This is going to be very easy for both of us. I've never been with a girl like you before but your beautiful and

117

I promise to treat you right. I've done some crazy shit for him before but he's never crossed the line."

Bo could feel me shaking. When we got into the elevator, he kissed me softly.

"Don't be scared," He said. "I'm not going to hurt you."

"What makes you think I'm scared?" I asked.

"I can feel you shaking," He replied "and I know this is your first real call."

I reached down and placed my hand on his crotch. I could feel his huge penis straining against the leather.

"Let's get something straight Bo. I'm not shaking because I'm scared. I'm shaking because I'm excited and because I can't wait to suck your cock until your head is spinning."

He smiled and squeezed my hand as the elevator doors opened.

"Good," he said, "then lets get this done."

CHAPTER 37

When it was over, after David has blown his load countless times on me and Bo, the two of us left David lying in the bed exhausted and went to take a shower.

"That was easier than I thought." Bo said.

We climbed into the shower together and began rinsing off. I felt nothing. I didn't feel cheap, I didn't feel broken. I certainly didn't feel like a victim. I was completely devoid of any real emotion which I thought at the time made it all the more okay. I never imagined for a moment that what I was doing now would begin to eat away at me later.

When we climbed out of the shower, Bo began drying me.

"I like you," he said. "I want to finish what we started. Just the two of us. Let's get high and fuck all night."

I looked at him and felt that familiar stirring. Pure animal lust. The way he looked in the soft light was heavenly...rippling muscles, a perfect cock so huge that even soft it hung halfway down his leg, that beautiful smile, the tattoos that covered his bicep...

"Why not?"

We left David asleep in the bed and went back to my room. We snorted coke all night and fucked over and over. He had never been with a transsexual before and every time the lights of the city illuminated my body, he would stare at my penis transfixed. His caress was tender and gentle. It had been completely different when we were with David. It was work. This time around it was just for us. We kissed passionately and when he pulled a condom over this throbbing shaft and flipped me on all fours, I didn't protest. I moaned and cried and screamed as he entered me. I loved it. He fucked me for over an hour. When it was over, I was exhausted. I fell asleep in his arms. When I woke up the next morning, he was gone.

I didn't have time to think about Bo one way or the other. He had left a note with an LA number on it and a message to call him when I woke up but David was already ringing my room. We spent the day shopping on Newberry Street. Then, dinner at a romantic restaurant in the North End, and finally a surprisingly easy and playful session afterward. As I was dressing to go back to my room, David took my hand.

"I want to see you again. Would you like that?" He asked.

"I would." I said it flippantly as though it meant nothing.

"I could arrange for you to see Bo again."

"Look David, lets get something straight. I don't need Bo to be with you. You're a very attractive and fascinating man. I enjoyed your company very much. This evening was perfect."

"I'll call Anthony. I have to be in Europe in a couple of weeks. I want you with me."

I smiled and kissed him on the cheek. The next day I flew back to Lauderdale, high on life and on coke, and I couldn't have been happier or more pleased with myself.

CHAPTER 38

When I returned to Lauderdale, I found no one waiting for me at the airport. I tried Jade's cell which kept going to voice mail. When I called the house, I reached one of the girls. She told me that a lot had happened over the weekend and that I should take a cab to the house right away. When I got there, everyone seemed to be milling around in a state of shock.

"What's going on?" I asked.

Kelly, a pretty Hispanic girl with amazingly hypnotic eyes was holding back her tears.

"Jade's dead," she replied.

"What?"

"Jade's dead. Overdose. Suicide. She swallowed a bunch of sleeping pills. Mia found her this morning."

I was stunned. Numb. I didn't know what to say or do. I couldn't even cry. It never occurred to me.

"How did this happen?" I asked.

"I just told you." Kelly finally broke down and fell right there on the floor. When I looked down upon her, she seemed so small and fragile, not at all like the confident, beautiful woman I knew. She continued sobbing and every time she spoke, she seemed to fall even deeper into despair. Finally, she collected herself and looked up at me.

"You know," she said, "There isn't even going to be a funeral. They just came and took her away while it was still dark outside so the neighbors wouldn't see."

"Who took her away?" I asked.

"Anthony and two of the security guys from the club."

"But what about her family?" I asked. "Shouldn't somebody call them?"

Kelly looked at me in amazement. There was venom in here eyes. Those beautiful eyes were filled with hate.

"Raquel," she said finally, "Anthony is her family. He's her father."

***

After Jade's death, everything changed. I found out that her real name had been Raquel and her father had initiated her into the "business" at a very early age. By the time she killed herself, she had been around the world three times and her spirit was completely broken. Her own father had pimped her out for profit. The savvy, classy business man was a monster. I finally saw him for what he was. Stripped of his money, his manners, the house, the cars, he was no better than a common criminal. In fact, he was worse. He was the most vile human being I had ever known. I was at a loss. Still reeling from the shock of her suicide, I decided to go home.

CHAPTER 39

Going home to my parent's house was considerably harder than I expected. After Anthony's muti-million dollar home, the cars, the shopping, the first class hotels and all the rest of it, Tampa and everything it represented seemed so small to me. My mom was happy to see me safe. My stepfather ignored me as usual. My sister was back at home having left her boyfriend of several years. My nephew was still adorable. Everything was exactly as I had left it. For some reason I couldn't wait to get out of there. It wasn't that I didn't love my family. It's that I felt apart from them. I wanted something very different for myself. That life seemed so bland. But I was happy to see them all, especially my mom. We sat up all night laughing and looking at all of my new clothes and shoes. It was the last time I remember her laughing, really laughing. She was sick. I could see it in her eyes.

She was now relying on medication to prolong the inevitable. She stared at the dresses and ran her fingers over the fine fabric, remembering her youth and her crazy glory days when she had worn sexy clothes and traveled the world with my father. Now she was sick and tired, a broken woman. Broken by circumstances beyond her control and broken by a horrible man that had simply destroyed her spirit. I couldn't stand to see her that way. It hurt. She had given up drinking which had been an escape for her. Now, there was no escape. The truth was there- staring her down like death itself and it wasn't pretty. She hated her life and what she had become. I promised myself that that would never happen to me. I would never look back in regret. I would never love or need a man so much that it compromised my happiness. She didn't ask what I was doing. She didn't have to. She did tell me that I had to be careful and that my happiness and safety was all that she cared about. The next morning, I took my mom shopping, to lunch, to a movie and then to buy groceries. I gave her five hundred dollars and told her to spend it on what she needed. That night, I packed an overnight bag and got on a plane to meet Jason. He was living in South Beach which at the time was the only place in the world to be and be seen. Every model, movie star, designer, rock star and artist was calling the once seedy enclave of Miami home. Jason had hooked up with a group of wealthy South American bodybuilders and male models. They were professional party boys who traveled the world in search of adventure. I told Jason I could only stay for the weekend. I stayed for three months.

CHAPTER 40

South Beach in the early late nineties was a mecca for the jet set and the beautiful people. When I stepped off the plane, Jason was there in all of his muscle bound glory to meet me. With him was an equally muscular, equally beautiful man he introduced as Sebastian. Sebastian and I hit it off immediately. You might even say it was love at first sight.

"Sophia, your going to love it," Jason said excitedly as we raced through the terminal. "The best clubs, the best beach, the best men, the best drugs."

"How long have you been here?" I asked.

"A month. I have to go back to get more clothes next week and then I'm coming back for the whole summer."

Sebastian squeezed my hand. "You should stay too," he said. "You can live with us at my place. There's plenty of room."

"I don't know, I have to be back in Boston soon and then I'm supposed to leave for Europe."

Sebastian smiled. God he was beautiful. Absolutely, undeniably perfect.

"Well the offer's good all summer," he said, "Come back anytime you want."

Sebastian's apartment was in the heart of South Beach and he shared the space with a muscular South American bodybuilder named Roman. He was handsome and sweet and I loved him immediately. One by one, the crew that would become my "family" for the summer began filing through the door and every man was more beautiful than the last. Richard, Eddie, Santiago, Juan. Everyone embraced me and welcomed me into the fold. Every woman in the world would have given her first born to be surrounded by the men that were in that room. Yes, they were gay. But they were also some of the most incredible looking men I would ever meet. I became their token "girlfriend." It was an unspoken rule that I should always be entertained and pampered. I was a queen, after all. The most beautiful one on the beach.

"We only have two rules here," Sebastian sang merrily. "You must put in at least one hour at the gym on a daily basis and no quitters. This is our time. Time for fun. Anything you need, ask me. Don't take the vials of GHB that are in the fridge. Those are for sale. Personal stash is in the closet, along with Tina (crystal meth) K (Ketamine- an animal tranquilizer that acts as a displacer) and X. Jason said you like coke but we'll break you of that habit. It's so eighties. Girl, it's dinosaur food. No body on the beach is doing that."

I laughed. I felt like Alice in Wonderland, just tumbling further and further into the rabbit hole. Needless to say, I didn't leave that weekend. I stayed all week and the week after, blowing off David's trip to Europe. I told Anthony that my mom was ill and I couldn't make it. He understood. Meanwhile, I partied my ass off. I did so much X over the course of that 10 days that I dropped twelve pounds. I didn't care. I was in love. In love with Sebastian, with Roman, with South Beach, with all of it. During the day we worked out or hit the nude beach where I paraded around topless with the hottest guys in Miami, half of whom I was waking up to every morning. At night, we had carte blanche at every gay and straight nightclub and total access to VIP area's usually restricted to and reserved only for celebrities. The drugs we consumed were legendary and my knack for mixing substances that would knock an elephant on its ass became one of my more celebrated traits, second only to my beauty of course. I was a star on the beach. Not like Kitty Meow, Daisy or Paloma De Laurentis. They were the true drag diva's of the beach. But I was the transsexual goddess and everyone, even the other girls, adored me. One morning, after an unusually hard night of partying, while Jason and Sebastian and I had breakfast at The Eleventh Street Diner, I had an epiphany. The conversation went like this:

Me: Why don't I just move here. I can leave to work when I have to and just come back to you guys.

Jason: That's what we have been saying all along.

Sebastian: Honey, we want you with us and you know the boys will love it."

And that's how it happened. They were my escape. They were my escape from all of it- my sick mother, from my own insecurity, the memories of Jade, from everything else that was bothering me or going on inside of my head. Surrounded by my tribe of muscle boys, I felt like the perfect female and they facilitated the fantasy by feeding into it. I was always the most beautiful, the most real, the most feminine...or so they said. The drugs were a constant. Always there when being the hottest girl surrounded by the hottest men in the hottest city just wasn't enough to do it. My favorite drugs of choice were ecstasy and special k. I ate the X, snorted the K and off I would go toward space. When I ran out of money from too much shopping or partying, they paid for everything. When they ran out of money, they stripped, entered hot body contests or wrote home to their parents. If all else failed, they actually sold the drugs we didn't consume. I worked when I needed too which wasn't much that summer. I told Anthony I had to stay close to home because of my mom. He sent me to Boston once a month. I stayed for a week each time. I usually came back to Miami with thousands of dollars. With the exception of the money I sent home, I spent the rest on clothes and drugs. Over fifty thousand dollars gone just like that...in three short months. So what do I have to show for it? Memories that will last a lifetime provided my memory holds out. The satisfaction of knowing that I built a legend on that beach that persists to this very day. And if nothing else, I had and still have a closet most women would kill for. More Cavalli, more Versace, more Gucci, Dior and Louis Vuitton than any queen that ever existed. And that's got to count for something, right? Well, maybe not!

CHAPTER 41

"I need you back in Lauderdale. Hopefully your mom is a little better since one of the girls saw you rolling your ass off in South Beach a few days ago."

The voice that spoke to me on the other end of the phone line was abrasive. It was, of course, Anthony. My "agent" was tired of me blowing off thousands of dollars worth of "dates." Frankly, so was I. I was tired. I had been partying non stop for three months and I needed to get back to work and make some money. I needed to get back to Tampa and see my mom. I needed a lot of things. But first I needed to get out of bed. I got out of bed and tried to do so without waking Sebastian and Jason, both of whom were in bed with me. I started throwing my clothes into a suitcase. Then I hopped in the shower, did my hair and a line of crystal meth which I hated but I knew would wake me up. As I was exiting the apartment, I surveyed my little tribe of lost boys. They were strewn about everywhere, asleep on the couch, in other rooms, on the floor. I did love them but it was time to go. Anthony arranged for a car to pick me up outside the apartment. I left the boys a note saying I would be back for the White Party and went back to Lauderdale to plot my independence from the agency. I would settle for nothing less than a hundred percent profit. But first I had a few more things to do and a few more people to see. The first one was one of the most famous men in the world. And that kind of trick requires a certain amount of discretion.

***

"How discreet can you be?" Anthony asked me the day after I got back to the house.

"Very," I replied, "why?"

"Because I have a very important assignment for you. If you blow this in any way, we're both fucked. You follow directions and keep your mouth shut and I can get you $10,000.00 for one night."

I stared at him in wide-eyed amazement. I had become accustomed to making and blowing ten grand in a week. But ten grand in one night- the idea just floored me. It wasn't that long ago that I was dancing in a red neck bikini bar and sleeping on my girlfriends couch.

"Ten grand in one night?" I repeated.

Anthony nodded. His cold eyes were alive. In fact, he seemed quite happy and in very good spirits for a man that had just lost his eighteen year old daughter to suicide. He was such a pig. Still, I continued with my questions.

"How many clients would I have to do?"

"Just one," he replied. "He's famous...very famous."

I was immediately excited. "Who?"

(Now, before I go on, I must reiterate something. Many of the names, in fact all of the names of my clients- both past and present- have been changed to insure their anonymity. The celebrities that I played with were always very generous with me. I enjoyed many of the fringe benefits that went along with knowing them. I never made the mistake of becoming too familiar with or overly possessive of any of them , a mistake a lot of Anthony's girls were making at the time. I was the wild and exotic fantasy for the men who create fantasy- pure and simple. Anthony's roster was impressive. Rock stars, politicians, bored porn stars, actors...whenever they asked for "something different" I'm the one they got. Some were famous, some were has-beens, but nothing prepared me for the evening I spent with one of the funniest, kindest and sexiest men I have ever known. . ...)

Anthony studied me, weighing the pro's and cons of trusting me with such potentially damaging information. Then he spoke.

"If I trust you with this information, with this client, I expect absolute discretion. Meaning, no one will know. Not your friends, your family, your mother and especially the other girls. You have to understand that if any paper gets a hold of this story, a man's career, his marriage, his life, is ruined. It's finished. He's not just a celebrity. He is my friend. He is a good guy. Can I trust you?"

"Of course," I replied quickly.

"Sophia, I need to be certain that I can trust you."

Anthony had not used my real name since I began work as "Raquel." I knew, by the menacing look in his eyes and the seriousness of his tone, that he meant business.

"Anthony, I replied, "I just want the ten grand. If he's famous, even better but my priority is the money. I'm not interested in wrecking a man's career."

"Good," he said, "Then go get ready. A limo will be here in two hours to take you to south beach. Your going to The Delano. The chauffeur will escort you upstairs to the penthouse. Security is expecting you. Look sexy but classy. Take something more risqué to change into. Be nice but give him what he wants…"

"Who is it?" I asked again.

"You'll see," was his final reply.

CHAPTER 42

When I walked into The Delano trailed by the chauffeur and a 350 lb security guard, you would have thought I was the superstar, although I must admit, I looked every inch the part. My dramatic, smoky make-up and slicked back hair went splendidly with the amazing backless Versace dress I had chosen to wear. They moved me swiftly through the lobby and ushered me into a private elevator. No one said a word. I still didn't know who I was about to meet. I felt as though I were about to crawl out of my skin with anticipation. Even the coke I had done before leaving the house couldn't cut the anxiety. I needed a drink...bad. The penthouse suite was magnificent. There was a bottle of champagne on ice and I decided to help myself.

"Make yourself comfortable," the security guy said. "He'll be with you in a moment. I need to see your purse."

"My purse? Why?"

"I need to check for recording devices or camera's."

"Your kidding?"

The 350 lb 6 foot 5 bear of a man looked at me with a sheepish grin. "Do I look like I'm kidding sweetheart?"

I handed him the purse. He fished through it for a moment, gave it back and smiled.

"All good," he said as he and the chauffeur walked out of the room.

I tried to relax as I waited but the anticipation was killing me. When I heard the footsteps behind me, I hesitated and turned slowly. It was surreal. There he was...one of the most famous faces in the world...standing right there in front of me. We'll call him "Jessie." He stood there, sizing me up. This man- this star of stars-perhaps the greatest comedic talent of his generation- just looking at me in awe. He looked exactly as he had on screen. He was dark and handsome with surprisingly expressive eyes. His smile could light up a room but I could see that he was as nervous as I was and his smile wasn't a comfortable one. I knew that it was up to me to break the ice and to do what I had to do to put him at ease.

"I understand that discretion is very important to you," I said.

He smiled but said nothing. I continued.

"I'm very pleased to be here with you. I'm a huge fan. I know that you have no reason to believe me but you can trust me. I wont do anything to make you feel uncomfortable and if I do, just tell me."

"Your very beautiful…" he said finally.

"Have you ever been with a girl like me before?" I asked.

"Yes," he replied, "but not as beautiful as you. Your truly amazing."

I smiled. "Can I pour you a glass of champagne?"

He walked toward me slowly.

"Do you kiss?" He asked.

"Not normally," I replied.

"Will you kiss me?" He asked.

"Yes," I replied.

He kissed me, softly at first then a little more aggressively but never forcefully. He was gentle. More importantly, he was behaving like a gentleman. He was nice.

"I have a great joke," he said suddenly, "would you like to hear it?"

I couldn't help but laugh. Here was one of the most famous comedians in the world asking me in the privacy of his hotel suite if he could do stand up for me.

"Of course," I replied.

So that's how he broke the ice. I laughed for what seemed like an eternity. Every time I thought he was through, he'd crack another joke. Soon, he was laughing and running around the room. He did characters, impersonations. He was electric…completely alive and at ease. By the time we finally sank into bed to make love, the sun was almost coming up….. He was massively endowed and didn't push the issue when I refused anal. When all was said and done, it really had been one of the most memorable evenings of my life. Though our relationship progressed slowly, I would continue to see him sporadically throughout that summer and early that fall. The sex was hot but more importantly, I laughed...He always made me laugh. And it was an especially confusing time in my life...and that's what I remember most about the time I spent with "Jessie".

CHAPTER 43

After "Jessie" all of my other calls seemed so boring. I was pretty much local for the next several weeks, seeing well-heeled clients in Palm Beach and The Keys. But nothing compared to the rush of being paid by a superstar. The rush of knowing that your wanted- desperately, passionately- by a man adored by millions. Well that is its own kind of drug. Not that I had given up the traditional kind. Far be it from me to refuse a bump. I remember that my addiction to cocaine was progressing quite nicely around that time. Every day, a bump here, a line there, you know, just to get me through it. I told myself it wasn't a problem as long as I could afford it. Not a problem when you're averaging three thousand dollars a day. Then one day it happened. The day that I was confronted full force by the sheer power of my addiction- my addiction to cocaine and to cold hard cash. It started out like any other day. I woke up, went to the gym with one of the girls, had lunch and went back to the house to meet my dealer and pick up my "assignments" for the evening. Anthony was already waiting

"Where have you been?" he asked.

"Out- why?" I replied.

"David's been waiting on Star Island for two hours for you to arrive. I told you about his party two days ago."

"Fuck," I muttered. "I completely forgot. I'll change."

Anthony had a cold look in his eyes.

"Next time I want you to keep your fucking cell phone with you...and you really should lay off the shit," he said before leaving the room.

I ran upstairs to change. I threw a few things into a Louis and went downstairs to greet David's driver. David was staying in a beautiful house on Star Island, a very wealthy enclave of Miami and home to some of the world's biggest stars including Sylvester Stallone. I had only seen him once since that crazy night in Boston with Bo. I didn't know what to expect. But I had been instructed that I wouldn't need a dinner dress so I assumed that we were staying in. Anthony had something about a "party" but I assumed that meant I would be working with a few of the other girls. The house was gated and sat directly on the water. It was a large Mediterranean style mansion that dwarfed even Anthony's rather impressive place. When I got to the atrium that preceded the front door, David was already waiting. He was as suave as ever. He was wearing a silk robe that seemed very reminiscent of Hugh Hefner.

"You look like a man with ten playmates waiting in the bedroom." I said with a laugh.

"Actually, a little more then ten," he replied.

He must have sensed my hesitation as he moved me toward the door.

"Raquel, are you all right?" he asked. His smile seemed sinister somehow. I knew I was in for something big. I refused to let the bastard get the best of me.

"I'm fine," I replied.

As we drew toward the door, I could hear voices. Many voices. Moans, Music. I couldn't distinguish what was real and what wasn't. The door was slightly ajar and opened to a hallway. Beyond, a huge sunken living room with a view of the ocean.

"I hope you ready for this," David said excitedly, "I have planned something very special for us."

The living room was almost completely empty with the exception of a huge movie screen and several fur throws and pillows on the floor.

"What a view," I said gazing out into the ocean.

"Look at this view," David commanded.

With that he fished a remote from his robe and the huge movie screen came alive with a very familiar face and a very familiar penis- It was Bo. It was one of his films. A bisexual orgy in which he simultaneously fucked both men and women. I smiled but said nothing. I was completely unprepared for what happened next. One by one, they began filing in. Fourteen men. Bo was there. So were several other men I recognized from adult films.

I turned to David.

"What is this?" I asked.

"This is what you would call a gang bang," David replied as though it were the most natural thing in the world.

I remembered Jade. She had always told me that remaining calm kept you in control. Losing your cool in a situation with more than one man could get you beaten or raped or both. I didn't want to be either.

I smiled and poured on the charm. I walked up to Bo and embraced him warmly. I smiled at the other guys, playfully grabbing their naked penises. Then I turned to David.

"David, can I see you for a moment before we get started?" I asked.

"Of course Raquel," He replied.

He led me toward a bathroom off the hallway. I remember that bathroom more clearly today than anything else that occurred. It was beautiful, all marble with a sunken roman tub and a steam shower. Mirrors wrapped around the entire room. There was cocaine cut neatly on gleaming trays.

I shut the door behind him and then I went off.

"What the fuck do you think your doing?" I asked

David was taken aback by my reaction. It was clearly unexpected.

"Raquel..." he began but I cut him off.

"You sorry mother fucker- you lured me here for this. You're no fucking gentlemen. You're a sick faggot who can't face his issues. You think I'm going to let fourteen guys run a fucking train on me for $1500.00? You're fucking crazy."

I was hysterical but managed to keep my voice low and controlled. We looked at each other for what seemed like an eternity. We sized each other up. For the first time, I think he saw the boy beneath the surface. The scrapper in me. I was ready to tear him a part.

"Maybe your right," he said finally, "Maybe that's exactly what I am. A faggot who wont face his issues. But I don't pay you to analyze me Raquel. I pay you to fuck me or fuck whomever I choose. Because that's what you do. You fuck people for money."

He was five seconds from an all out assault but I knew that I couldn't beat them all. He continued speaking.

"Now, we seemed to have gotten off on the wrong foot today and I still would like to make it up to you. Also, you seem to be under the impression that I wanted you to fuck all of these men for $1500.00 dollars. That's not correct. I want you to interact with them. All of them. Bo will be the only one fucking you...And I will pay $1500.00 for every man that's out there. So you do the math."

That's when I knew. This was it. The defining moment where I either said "No, enough is enough," or I agreed to cross the line and lose a part of myself forever. I stared at David with hatred in my eyes. I had never felt such contempt for any man other than my step father.

"I need a minute," I said finally.

"Take your time," he said quietly as he left the room.

I stared at myself in the mirror. I hated what I saw. I didn't know what to do. I wanted to scream, I wanted to cry, I wanted to run from that house and never look back...for a moment, I even wanted my mother. But IT was there too. The desire for money, the lure of the drugs cut out in front of me, the sexual hunger for all of those hot porn stars, especially Bo. There was a decanter of Dewars on the counter. I took it and drank straight from the bottle. Then I did four lines of cocaine. Then I took one more look in the mirror. Then I opened the door. When I walked in the guys were completely un-dressed and already involved in sexual acts of various natures. Bo was waiting for me with a sad look on his face. He hated it as much as I did. He smiled wearily as I approached him.

"Let's get this done," he said.

"Let's get this done," I replied.

***

When the little party was over and the men began dispersing, David told me where to find the money. I picked up my clothes and walked into the kitchen. I found the money and went back to the bathroom. Bo was there, doing lines off of the counter. I moved around him and got into the shower. The water felt ice cold even though it was burning hot. I could feel the tears streaming down my face. I felt dirty. Actually, dirty doesn't even begin to describe how I felt. I washed my hair and scrubbed my body for what seemed like hours. When I got out, Bo was sitting on the counter swigging Dewars from the bottle. I began drying off and pulled my hair back into a wet ponytail.

"Do you want to go somewhere?" He asked, "I'm still pretty fucked up."

"No, I'm going home." I replied. "I've had just about enough of this shit."

It was then that I noticed Bo looking at himself in the mirror. He seemed very distant. He turned to me and asked me if he looked old. I didn't answer. I threw my clothes on and had David's driver take me straight to the airport. That night, I took the last flight back to Tampa. I flew first class one way. My hair was soaking wet. I was coming down from the cocaine. I felt miserable. In my Louis Vuitton bag I had one pair of shorts, some lingerie and twenty one thousand dollars in cash. I cried the whole way.

CHAPTER 44

I slept for three straight days when I got to Tampa. My mom woke me occasionally to make sure I ate something but other than that, she left me alone. She didn't ask what was wrong. But she knew something terrible had happened. She offered the kind of quiet support I needed at the time. I was in a kind of ask me no questions, I'll tell you no lies state of mind. Just as well. We were both hiding a kind of truth from each other- I refused to discuss my work, my addictions and all the rest of it- she refused to discuss her health which was failing considerably.

I stayed in Tampa for a few days, eventually falling back into my familiar pattern of late nights and constant partying. I briefly met up with Sierra and we had some great times at a new rave that was taking Tampa by storm- The Fantasy Ranch. But the lure of Sobe was calling and one of the largest circuit parties in the world was just a few days away, The White Party. The White Party was a three day drug-filled odyssey that culminated with my twenty fifth birthday. My boys were ecstatic to have me home and for awhile, they and the drugs we consumed, were able to help me forget about David and that horrible day on Star Island. I remember very little about the parties...there were several over the course of the weekend. I slept very little, if at all. I ate less. I ingested so much ecstasy at one point that my hands would not stop shaking. Even after I threw up several times, I still went looking for more. Not one of my so called friends told me stop. They couldn't- they were too fucked up to notice. As the weekend dragged on, I hooked up with one of the official White Party Dancers who had flown into Miami with superstar DJ Junior Vasquez. He was a beautiful, muscular Puerto Rican with a huge cock and a seemingly never ending supply of drugs which of course meant that he was my new best friend.

The White Party, with all of its glamorous seediness and debauchery, did serve one other purpose other than providing a decadent setting in which to celebrate my birthday. It was instrumental in my evolution from notorious south beach party girl to working model. It was at The White Party that I met a photographer named Pasquale Devane. Devane was much older than me, gay and extremely European. He caught me at the tail end of the party and although I had been up for three days and was so high I couldn't remember my name, he took an instant shine to the beautiful transsexual cavorting on the dance floor in a see-through white bodysuit. He was with a group that included several well known European model types and hanger-on's. I noticed them chatting amongst themselves and when he noticed me noticing them, Pasquale motioned me over.

"What is your name?" he asked

"Sophia," I replied.

The group studied me for a moment and then they all nodded in unison.

"Sophia," Pasquale said, "I am a photographer and these are a few of the people that I have gathered to participate in a project that I am doing in Greece. We would like you to be a part of it. Would you come to Europe with us?"

I looked around the room- which was spinning- and thought about all the other prospects that were waiting for me- more drugs, more tricks, more clothes, more clubs. I was feeling a bit over it. I was in the mood for something new and I had plenty of money so I didn't need to work.

"Why not," I replied.

Two days later, knowing very little about Pasquale Devane, I boarded a first class flight to Athens.

CHAPTER 45

The transcontinental flight started out on the wrong foot almost immediately. Before we reached the security check point Pasquale announced to no one in particular that if anyone had drugs we had exactly five minutes to dispose of them.

"I don't want anyone fucked up in my presence. That's why we went to The White Party. The party is over. It's work time. Get rid of it."

One of the male models, a skinny but beautiful boy named Marcos, quickly went to the bathroom to dispose of the blow he had generously shared with me in the limo before we picked up Pasquale. Pasquale then turned his attention toward me.

"Sophia, be a dear and dispose of whatever you have."

"I don't have anything," I said.

He smiled. "Let's hope not. I don't want to start off on the wrong foot."

I excused myself and headed toward the news stand announcing that I would have to have something to read if I was to survive the flight. What I really needed was water. Even though it was 9:00 am and I hadn't had a thing to eat, I had no intention of disposing of my last hit of X in such a horrendous manner as flushing it. I would take it. I would roll all the way to Greece and no one would know. I was a professional partier. I could handle this. I quickly and discreetly fished the X out of my purse and swallowed it. Since it normally takes about 30 to 45 minutes for X to take effect, I assumed I would have enough time to make it through security and more than likely on to the plane. Of course, I was wrong. It was particularly strong X. It took effect quite quickly and by the time our little group reached the gate, I was rolling my ass off. Marcos, on the other hand, seemed even sketchier, more pre-occupied with rummaging through his backpack.

I realized that we had both done the same thing. I had taken the last of my drugs and he had done all of his coke. He was wired for sound. If Pasquale noticed, he didn't say anything. He said very little on the flight. Marcos did most of the talking, of course. I, in my state of eternal techno bliss, spent most of the time clinging to one of the gorgeous female models. Her name was Thalia. If she minded, she didn't show it. She just smiled and held my hand tightly. Thalia was like a Sierra. She was dark and beautiful but somehow different. I couldn't put my finger on it. As she spoke, I studied her. I studied the group I had suddenly and inexplicably taken off to Europe with. Strangers all, but nice enough. They each had their own unique and exotic beauty. Thalia was beautiful but mysterious. Marcos was handsome but feminine. All of the others too, seemed to have an androgynous quality about them- a strange but spellbinding mix of both male and female. When I mentioned this to Pasquale, he smiled and said something I will always remember.

"Beauty," he said, "should never be ordinary. Not if it's meant to be relevant."

I thought about that simple comment and how wise he seemed. Honestly, he had told me very little about the project. It was to be called *Xotica: A Thing Of Beauty*. Pasquale was a photographer, very avant garde and glamorous. He enjoyed photographing "that which was different." He believed that in order to live, one must truly experience life. Beauty he insisted was fleeting. But through the camera, he could capture it and keep it forever. The purpose of this current project was very personal to him and would eventually become a tribute to a very dear friend who was dying of AIDS. I was extremely excited. I trusted Pasquale immediately. I know that looking back, it seems crazy that I just allowed myself to be swept away by a group of strangers. But hey- this was life in the fast lane. This was South Beach in the nineties. Instant friendships are formed and before you know it your on a first class flight to Europe with some very interesting people. Eventually, the X wore off and Thalia and I ended up cuddling and sleeping through the duration of the flight. When I woke up, the plane was circling the Athens airport and everyone was chatting excitedly. I remember thinking that this would be the greatest experience of my life. For the first time, in a long time, without the help of drugs, I was completely and truly happy.

***

The Greek Islands. How do I describe one of the oldest places on earth? One of the most breathtakingly beautiful places on the planet. I cannot. It is impossible to comprehend without seeing them firsthand. From the night clubs and café's of Mykanos, to the ruins and splendor of Santorini, to the beaches of Crete. It is the one place every person should visit at least once in their life, if given the chance. I was completely awestruck by Athens. We had a few hours to kill before catching the boat to Santorini, the island that would serve as home base for the next two months. Pasquale, who was Greek and Spanish, had grown up in Athens. He was barely out of his teens when he moved to France to study photography. It was there that he adopted the more glamorous last name of Devane. He knew Athens well. We covered the basics with what little time we had. By the time we boarded the boat for Santorini, I was elated. All thoughts of drugs had been erased from my thoughts. I was a part of something substantial and I was determined to make the most of it. I was high on the country, the people, the sea that stretched out before us. It was intoxicating. Greece had a strange and sobering effect on me. A humbling effect. I was ready to begin this new and exciting adventure.

CHAPTER 46

Xotica was to feature seven young models.

Nia: A beautiful 18 year old transsexual from France. She was petite and blonde with small breasts.

Candace: A beautiful lesbian with a shaved head and a scorpion tattoo on her back.

Anthony & Rocco: Twin brothers- both stunning northern Italian Gods with incredible faces and amazing bodies.

And of course the beautiful Thalia, the oh-so pretty Marcos and myself. Pasquale had rented an amazing home for the length of our stay. We were on one of the more private parts of the island and the villa was built into a cliff and overlooked the sea. We had a huge verandah with a plunge pool. There were several bedrooms and Pasquale instructed us to pair off and to leave the large master for him. The brothers took one room, Nia and Candace took another and Thalia and Marcos and I agreed to share a large king sized bed in a room with the most amazing view , to this day, I have ever seen. Pasquale had warned us that we would be roughing it a bit. He wanted us to develop a closeness, a camaraderie thus the reason for the somewhat cramped sleeping arrangement. It was imperative to the nature of the project that we appear to be best friends, lovers, playmates and singular individuals. He in no way encouraged sexual interaction in front of or behind the camera. He wanted erotica and sensuality, not sex. He shot me first, alone and helped me get comfortable in front of the camera. Thalia watched in the background offering tips on movement. They encouraged me to use my eyes, my lips, my hands in very slow erythematic ways. He shot about two rolls of test shots. The real shoot would begin tomorrow and progress over the course of our stay. It never occurred to me that Pasquale had brought me here without photographing me first. Most photographers insist on a test shoot before a project. It's crucial. Many beautiful people don't photograph well at all. But something inside of him must have known. He told me later, "I just believed in you. From the moment I saw you. Dancing, surrounded by all those beautiful men, every one of them in love with you. You had a magic about you. I knew you were going to be someone very special."

Pasquale stayed up most of the night developing my pictures in a makeshift dark room he had created. He had photographed everyone in the group before so he wanted to be sure of my strengths and weaknesses by the time morning came. The rest of us went out to explore the island and eventually ended up in a little bar called Paracas. We were definitely curiosities to the locals. As individuals, each of us had a striking beauty. Together, we seemed almost surreal. Over the course of the evening and several pitchers of wine, we became very friendly and got to know each other. We danced with several of the patrons and with each other and laughed and sang joyously with the band. All in all, it was one of the happiest nights of my life. When it was over, we stumbled back to the villa, a little drunk, and sank into bed. Thalia and Marcos and I fell asleep in each others arms like old friends. The sound of waves crashing against the cliff lulled me to sleep. The morning was just hours away...

***

Pasquale was elated with my test shots. Needless to say, I was a natural in front of the camera and extremely photogenic. That morning we started out for one of the Greece's most famous spots, Akrotiri. It was crowded but we managed to find a hidden cove that allowed us the seclusion that Pasquale was searching for. Pasquale had hired a local boy to assist with the camera equipment and to carry the bag that contained the costumes we would be using for the day's shoot. His name was Andreas and he was amazingly youthful and sexy. I had decided then and there that he would be my lover- at least for as long as I was in Greece. The first shoot seemed stiff. I wasn't comfortable and couldn't figure out why. Pasquale was patient and with Thalia's

help, I began to ease into it. By the end of the day, I would be trans-
formed from a pseudo model into an exotic goddess- dripping wet in
a dress made entirely of white pearls- with one of the most spectacular sunsets as a backdrop. Pasquale would laugh and cry out joyously
whenever I did something he "loved." When he wrapped my set, I
flirted innocently with Andreas as Pasquale shot the twins. It wasn't
long before I found my attention drawn to Anthony and Rocco. The
twins, both naked, lounged in each others arms against the rocks.
The water splashed against them and their dreamy eyes seemed as
far away as the sun. Their non sexual interaction still seemed vaguely
erotic to me. Their bronzed sculpted bodies, their perfectly identical
perfect faces...It was one of the most beautiful if not homo erotic
images I had ever seen and the style in which he shot them precipi-
tated the Abercrombie & Fitch ad's by several years. He was a master
and very ahead of his time. Like Andy Warhol, Pasquale lived only
for the art, the image. Xotica was to be his most personal work and
his swan song. Of course, we didn't realize at the time that we were a
part of something very special and artistic. That would come much
later. That day and on the days that followed, he shot us as individuals, paired off and together as a group- laughing, playing, swimming,
sleeping, dancing, dreaming.

As the project came together, there were haunting black and
white images of the twins staring into each others eyes- into each other's very souls. There were images of me and Marcos at sunset—naked
and sharing a martini. Thalia's beautiful face stared back from several
stark stills, her eyes deep and soulful, her lips parted just perfectly so.
There were pictures of us on the beach, in the villa, dancing under the
stars. My favorite- a photo that Pasquale would later call "SEVEN"-
featured all of us asleep in each others arms. I am between the twins,
their strong arms cradling me in a passionate embrace. To me, the
image seemed to capture us at our most real and our most vulner-
able. "SEVEN" was all the more powerful and provocative when you
consider the relationships that can form- the human bonds that can
come- when even complete strangers find themselves desperately and

passionately in need of *SOMETHING*. I'm not sure what the others were searching for. I'm not sure if I found what I was looking for on that sun drenched island. But Pasquale knew we were searching and for a brief moment he captured that yearning, that longing in all of us- on film...and it was magical.

CHAPTER 47

Our time in Greece sped by before any of us knew what was happening. We had lived, played and laughed together. The eight of us truly felt like a family. With the exception of alcohol, I had been clean for two months.

I had been a significant part of something monumental. As we boarded the plane for America, a quiet sadness had settled upon the group. We had all exchanged address information at the Villa and promised to stay in touch but I think we all knew that life would probably make that impossible for most of us. We were each from different places- geographically as well as mentally. If Pasquale had not hand picked us, we may have never had the privilege of knowing each other. It was a long flight. We slept most of the way. By the time we reached America, we were all to tired to cry. We said our goodbye's and that was it. The twins went one way, Thalia the other way and so on and so on until I found myself alone with Pasquale watching them all disappear into the crowd. We looked at each other wistfully.

"So, where will you go now Sophia?" Pasquale asked.

I shrugged.

"Honestly, I'm not sure." I replied. "Maybe back to the beach or home for awhile."

Pasquale looked at me. His eyes were kind and when he took me in his arms his embrace was fatherly and heartfelt.

"Never, let anyone make you feel as though you are less than a woman," he said. "You are more than one. You are beauty. You have an amazing presence, in front of the camera and in life."

He continued...

"The sad thing about the world Sophia is that most people lack vision and tolerance of anything other than what they consider normal...and make no mistake...normal is ORDINARY! Ordinary is never exciting no matter how you try to package it. Ordinary is dull and lifeless and lacks relevance. ORDINARY SUCKS!"

I smiled. I didn't want to let him go. I felt as though he had so much to teach me.

He embraced me once more and turned away. I watched him go. Though he and I would continue to correspond until his death through letters, email and phone calls, I would never see Pasquale Devane again. He was a visionary. He was a man that sacrificed the promise of mainstream success by staying true to himself. He was the quintessential artist that never sold out. He was a painter but it was his photographs- stark and true- that he wanted to be remembered by. I will always remember him as a man of great beauty and knowledge with the uncanny ability to see the sadness in someone and make it beautiful again.

CHAPTER 48

"Mom is really sick. You need to come home." The voice that spoke to me on the phone was stressed, agitated and belonged to my sister, Josette. I had returned to the South Beach apartment instead of going home as I should have. I knew my mother's condition was getting worse. She had cirrhosis of the liver. Even though she hadn't touched a drink in a couple of years, years of abusing alcohol had destroyed her. I was scared to face her. I didn't want to lose my mother. What my mother and my sister didn't realize was that I had run and kept running not because I didn't love them- but because I couldn't deal with THAT LIFE anymore. The sadness, the despair and the sickness that enveloped that little house in west Tampa was stifling. It always had been. But like it or not, I knew my mother needed me. I would be there. I had not been there much- with the escorting and traveling and partying- but I vowed I would be there now. So in the early morning hours of a particularly rainy morning in Miami, I boarded a plane for Tampa.

After Europe and the glamour of my life in Miami, Tampa was worse than death. By the time I got home, I found myself wondering what all the fuss had been about. My mother met me at the airport and she seemed fine. She didn't look her best but overall, she seemed okay. She explained that she had her good days and her bad days. She asked me not to leave again. I promised I wouldn't. Though my mother asked me to move into the house, I couldn't. I couldn't stand the sight of my stepfather. I loathed him. I found a small loft apartment and decorated it lavishly with the rest of the twenty one thousand dollars I had left. Now that I was broke, I was faced with the monumental task of trying to find a way to earn a living. I had lost touch with Anthony after leaving for Europe and just as well since my mother's illness made it impossible for me to travel. A desk job was completely out of the question as was anything in the retail, food or "typical" service industry. I had been hearing a lot about the money that could be made on the internet. I had even been offered contracts to pose exclusively for adult websites based in south Florida. I called my old boyfriend Andrew and though he had absolutely no reason to want to help me, he loaned me twenty thousand dollars to research and build a website. I called Pasquale and although the internet was still a relatively new medium to him, he offered a few choice words of wisdom.

"Don't be trashy. The world is full of trash. It stinks and fucks up everything. You want to pose nude- fine. There is nothing wrong with your body. It's beautiful. But present it beautifully. Be proud of your body and let that show through. Think Playboy- not Hustler. If you need me, call me...You'll be great. Just believe that you will be and...You will be."

With the help of a team of highly skilled individuals, I set out to build the first true transsexual adult website with little or no focus on hardcore pornography. We worked for weeks. I lived on the computer, scanning the straight sites of former playboy playmates and internet glamour girls like Cindy Margolis. I avoided the transsexual sites like the plague. I wanted absolutely no influence in my design or construction of the site. I began shooting with several photographers, choosing key pictures that I thought represented what I was going for. I began building a portfolio. I spent thousands of dollars and many hours in front of the camera for just a few perfect shots. When I wasn't working on the site, I spent time with mom or Lissette. It was so good to see Lissette again. She was more beautiful than ever. She was happily involved in a relationship and I was happy that she was happy. About a week before my site went online, my mother went in to the hospital. She remained there for three days. She was weak. She was dying. Family that had avoided her for years now came flooding back into her life. The absent brother, the cousins who rarely called- suddenly they were all there to share the burden of this enormous loss. Never mind that they didn't want to be a part of her life. They absolutely had to be a part of her death. How familial- to cry and comfort each other as one of your own slips away- What a bunch of fucking hypocrites they all were. I had no use for any of them, still don't. When she left the hospital, she went back to my sister's home to recuperate. She never really made it through the night. By morning, she was lapsing into coma. By the time the ambulance had reached the hospital, she was already gone. My sister, Lissette and I were there together. Just the three of us- alone in the hospital- when the doctor told us that she had passed. Mom's three favorite girls. She wouldn't have wanted it any other way. The funeral was small and mostly family. My uncle and many of my relatives ignored me. They never told me they were sorry for my loss though they all held and comforted my sister. It was so typical. I sat in the pew with Jason and Lissette and Lissette's mother. They were the ones that offered words of comfort and sympathy as the tears fell silently and continuously down my face. Aside from my sister and her in laws who were also very kind to me, Lissette and Jason were my family now. The rest of them could all go fuck themselves!

CHAPTER 49

My mother's death and my guilt over not spending more time with her toward the end of her life, sent me into the most self destructive tail spin I have ever known. Three days after her funeral, I tracked down Tish , Sierra and several other people I hadn't seen in awhile. They were moving in totally different circles now and the crew they were running with threw parties of legendary proportions, many of which went on for several drug fueled days.

I was there for every one of them. My first one went on for two and half days. No sleep, no food. Just cocaine, X, GHB, Special K and water when I needed it. I even snorted heroin but it made me sick and I never touched it again. By the time I had recovered from that one, there was another in the works and I was there for that one too...and so on and so on until my mother's death and everything else in my life had absolutely no meaning any more. I was completely numb. The drugs were always a social thing for me. I never went home and partied alone. When I was at home, I worked on my website which was at the time still in the beginning stages of development although I was already online and getting considerable traffic. To complicate matters further, my father- my real father, the one I had not seen since I was fourteen years old- was being released from prison after nearly thirty years and wanted desperately to see me. My father first went to prison during my lifetime when I was six months old. By all accounts, he was a career criminal. He ran with the Italian/Irish bad boys of Vegas and New Orleans...a good old goodfella if ever there was one. Until he was released from prison shortly after my twenty sixth birthday, I had not seen him in over a decade. His career as a criminal consisted mostly of some small time stuff and more importantly, big money heists. But what ultimately sent him to prison for thirty years besides the obvious was my father's uncanny ability to escape from maximum security prisons. Three bullets in his left leg during his final and only unsuccessful attempt put an end to his shenanigans but his time was tripled on account of them. When an obscure law was amended, granting freedom to several hundred long-term Florida inmates, my father- outside for the first time in two decades- found himself at my sister's doorstep. Josette, always the trooper, took him in.

Explaining to your father that his son is now a beautiful woman came considerably easy to my sister. She always had that ability. The ability to just say what you feel- straight out- come what may. He was, surprisingly, very understanding. My sister assured me that he wanted to see me. We agreed to meet the following night.

I must have turned my car around three times on the way to her house. I couldn't believe how nervous I was. When I finally made it to the front door, it was nearly 10:30 pm and I had told them that I would be there at 8:00.

We stared at each other for a full minute before he finally reached out to touch me and I him. It was an odd, clumsy embrace but ultimately it gave way to mutual longing- almost clinging in it's intensity. He broke down, weeping uncontrollably for about ten minutes. I remained surprisingly cool and calm. I knew then that this was the moment I had been waiting for all of my life. The love- in fact, the very existence- of *HIM*. We sat down and in one hour I tried to explain all that had happened in my life in the last 12 years. It was a futile attempt at closeness. Though I knew in my heart his love was genuine, I still could not help but feel a sense of detachment, more on my part than his. Over the course of several months, we tried to develop a sense of family. He called often. I made him dinner. We went shopping. But there was a wall that I just would not allow him to penetrate. He knew it. After awhile, he stopped trying. I couldn't blame him. It was an impossible feat. I believed as I always had that life would have been better- different- if he had been a part of it. I know now that that just wasn't the case. The cruel irony of it all was that he truly was offering me the one thing I wanted more than anything- *HIS love*. I didn't take it. If I allowed myself the luxury of regret, I would regret that most of all. He died a few months later of cancer knowing he had tried- but failed- to reach me.

CHAPTER 50

Charlie. Of all the memories that I have written about, the ones associated with this man have been the most joyous and the most painful to relive. Words cannot begin to describe what an extraordinary individual he was and how he changed me and my perception of love, forever. Charlie as you probably remember from previous chapters was my Candy man, the handsome stranger from Tracks and a man that for some odd reason, continued to pop up at various places in various stages of my life- some not touched on in this book. Our meetings were always brief but the passion between us was undeniable. Unlike most men who came face to face with my astonishing physical firepower, Charlie never tried to sleep with me. He was flirtatious but never vulgar. He was confident but never cocky. He was sweet but never overbearing. He was the perfect combination of smoldering sensuality and the boy next door. He also had the most perfectly handsome face I had ever seen on a man and I melted each and every time I looked into those deep chestnut eyes.

Note to Reader: Right Now your thinking, "Come on Sophia, cut the crap. This guy sounds too good to be true."

Truth is, he was too good to be true. Charlie was a very complicated man and to pigeonhole him would be impossible. He was many things to many people. At times, he was even different with me. But throughout the course of a long and very dramatic relationship, I believe he taught me how to love. This is not a comment that I make lightly so please pause collectively, dear reader, and give this comment the respect that it deserves. This man taught me how to love. Unconditionally, without fault and with a passion so intense that it haunts me to this very day. So now I will begin at the beginning which was not the beginning of us but was by all accounts and purposes, the beginning of our life together.

CHAPTER 51

I was high on cocaine and ecstasy. I was dancing- barely standing actually- when he saw me. Again. It was a Friday night in Tampa and I was at a gay club called Rascal's with some of my friends doing my usual- looking fabulous, getting high, trying to exist. My friends were pressuring me to leave but I would hear nothing of the sort. Good luck in getting me out of a club when I was rolling. So I danced, alone, all eyes on me...it was an electrifying feeling. It always had been. Now, even more so, because my look had changed a bit. With the money my website had begun to generate I had pulled a little nip and tuck with one of the country's finest plastic surgeons. I had enlarged my breasts yet again and my newly enhanced 34DD bustline on my five foot eight inch, 115 pound frame was nothing short of traffic stopping. Never one to push the envelope surgically, I had enhanced my lips, nose and cheekbones but retained a very natural look. I had also vetoed all suggestions of silicone injections in my hips and ass area, a decision that I am still thankful for today. My body was tight, firm and athletic. By all accounts, by the time we found each other again, my look had completely evolved. I was the Raquel Reyes that you see in front of you today. He couldn't take his eyes off of me. In my drug induced haze, I could barely see him. My friends, insistent that we go club hopping in Ybor, finally pushed me toward the door. He moved through the crowd and planted himself directly in my path, stopping me dead in my tracks.

"Hi Sophia," He said.

"Oh my God...Charlie," I replied. "How are you?"

"I'm good. I was hoping I would see you here. I just moved back from Lauderdale and I'm living in South Tampa now."

He may as well have been speaking Japanese. Though my head was suddenly clear, I was too wrapped up in that beautiful face to pay any attention to what was coming out of his mouth. It had been nearly eight years since we'd met and he still had that irresistible effect on me. Aside from looking a little skinnier than I remembered him, he still looked the same and that was damn good. I told my friends that I wasn't going anywhere.

That night we danced, high on ecstasy and each other, until the wee hours of the morning. He was the most magnetic man I had ever known. When he kissed me- really kissed me for the first time- I trembled. I had never wanted- needed- someone more in my life. I begged him to take me home and make love to me.

"If I make love to you tonight," he said, "I'm not leaving tomorrow. I don't want a one night stand."

I weighed those words. I couldn't have been happier.

"Neither do I," I replied.

By the time we made it back to my apartment the sun was coming up and the ecstasy had worn off. It didn't matter. We made love all afternoon and I felt higher than any drug had ever made me feel. He was the perfect lover. Gentle when I needed him to be. Rough when I wanted him to be. He was completely at ease with my body and his soft whispers in my ear drove me absolutely crazy. By the time he fell asleep, I was completely exhausted and totally in love. I closed my eyes, his strong arms cradling me. This is it, I told myself. This is the one. This is the one I'll love forever.

CHAPTER 52

The next morning, Charlie woke up early and took my car to the market. He came back with an array of pastries and bagels and freshly squeezed juice. Then we sat down at the table to get to the bottom of our little fascination with each other and where- if any- where- it would lead us. Charlie did most of the talking. I knew that if I opened my mouth I may find myself saying something horribly irrational like- "I love you, I've always loved you." So I bit down on my lip and prayed for silence.

"Sophia," he said pointing to his head. "You have always been right here. Always on my mind. Why do you think that is?"

"Honestly," I replied, "I don't know. But I feel the same way. I've never had a stronger reaction to any man in my life. Every time I see you is like the first time. I will never forget that first time- what you wore, how you looked. You stayed with me."

I paused.

"You know," I said finally, "I've fantasized about you...many times."

He smiled.

"I can't tell you how many times I've thought about you over the years- sexually and otherwise," he said laughing.

"Why did it take so long for us to get to this point?" I asked. "Why did it take so long for you to make love to me when you knew you could have had me that first night...and all of the other nights over the years?"

He thought for a moment and finally spoke.

"Because, that wouldn't have been making love. It would have been fucking. I didn't want to fuck you. I wanted to make love to you and hold on to you for as long as I could. That's why I waited. Because

I wanted you to be something different...someone special to me and I wanted to be that for you."

I processed his words. The sincerity that poured from him was honest. He spoke slowly and chose his words carefully. He wanted to get his point across. He wanted to affect me. Before I realized what was happening, it began to fade. My resolve, my imperviousness, that great steel wall surrounding my heart began melting away.

I cried. I cried the most real tears I have ever cried in the presence of another human being. They were tears of sadness, despair, loss...and of hope.

"I'm so lonely," I admitted to him as he took me in his arms.

"Not anymore," he said softly, "Not anymore."

And that was how it happened. That was how we fell in love. He never left my side. We went everywhere, did everything together. He was an amazing cook and every night he treated me to something new and exotic.

I fell asleep in his arms- always assured in my belief that he would be there when I woke up...and he was.

His smiling, gorgeous face. His dancing eyes. It was the happiest time of my life. There was no reason to believe that it would ever change.

CHAPTER 53

"Sophia, wake up. Please wake up. I need to go to the hospital."

Charlie's voice was urgent and desperate as he roused me from my sleep. I looked at the clock on the bedside table. It was 4:30 am.

"What's wrong?" I asked.

"My priapism is at it again. It really hurts. I need to go to the ER."

Charlie had previously explained to me that because of a car accident he had been involved in South Florida- one in which he was struck as a pedestrian by a moving truck and thrown several hundred feet- he suffered from a rare but debilitating and extremely painful condition known as priapism. Doctors aren't sure why and when priapism can occur though it's often attributed to people with spinal injuries, paraplegics, cocaine addicts and those suffering from sickle cell anemia. It is a condition that occurs when all of the blood rushes to the penis- the penis becomes swollen and engorged and unable to become flaccid without medical attention or immediate medication, can be one of the most painful experiences a man can endure. I know it sounds preposterous but it is a legitimate medical condition. I had gone to the internet when he had first informed me of it. After much searching I found a brief reference of the problem in the John Hopkins Medical Journal.

So there I was- half asleep at 4:30 am- with a large hard penis in my face- and for the first time in my life- I didn't know what the hell to do with it. Charlie was obviously in excruciating pain. He was practically doubled over on the floor. I jumped out of bed and tried to help him put his clothes on. His entire body was shaking. He was near screaming by the time I got him to my car. When we reached the hospital, the nurse on duty remembered him from a previous episode. Apparently, the hospital in Tampa knew very little about the problem and had consulted a specialist when he had been brought in the first time. She tried to talk him through the pain while she pulled up his insurance information. Then she quickly rushed him back to the ER. He was holding my hand tightly and screaming for pain medication.

The nurse tried to calm him down, speaking softly as she readied his meds. "Charlie, I'm going to have administer this directly into your penis. It's neosynephren. It's going to stop the swelling. It's going to hurt."

I tried to turn away but Charlie held tightly to my hand. I hated needles. There was no way I could watch this nurse stick one in his penis. I struggled to free myself but he wouldn't let go.

"Charlie, you've got to be still," The nurse pleaded. "I know it hurts but I have to be very careful when I administer this. Please stop moving."

"Charlie, please let me go," I whispered as the nurse moved toward his penis with the needle. "I cant watch this."

"No, don't go," he begged.

I tried to jerk my hand away but the nurse was having none of it. She fixed a cold stare on me. "Stop moving," she commanded.

It was no use. I couldn't escape. I closed my eyes as she stuck the needle into his penis and injected the liquid furiously. The scream that escaped from his lips was wrenching. Then completely covered in sweat, exhausted and in pain, he let go of my hand and passed out. I sank down on the floor next to his bed. My mind was blank. I couldn't believe what I had just witnessed. What the hell had I gotten myself into?

CHAPTER 54

They admitted Charlie into the hospital later that morning. They called in his specialist who evaluated his condition and offered two options.

1) Operate. The procedure would relieve him of all pain but render him impotent before the age of thirty.

Or

2) Charlie could learn to administer the neosynephren himself and inject his own penis whenever he had an episode.

Hmmm…something to think about. He wasn't even thirty years old and he was in the midst of a life changing medical condition. The doctor informed Charlie that he was going to keep him in the hospital for about a week to observe and chart his condition. In the meantime he prescribed a very strong pain medication and left instructions for one of the male nurses to teach Charlie the proper way to use the needle on his penis. I stood quietly off to the side of the room. Finally we were alone. He looked over at me sheepishly.

"I'm so sorry," he began to apologize but I cut him off immediately with a soft kiss.

"It doesn't matter," I said. "I'm here for you. This doesn't matter."

He looked at me for what seemed like an eternity. Then he took me in his arms and said it. He didn't whisper it or mumble it or say it in the way that most men do when they're trying to make light of it. He said it clearly. He said "I love you."

"I love you too," I replied.

That was it. That's where it happened. In a hospital room at Tampa General Hospital, I gave into my feelings and admitted to him that I loved him. More importantly, I admitted it to myself and that changed everything.

CHAPTER 55

Over the course of Charlie's stay in the hospital, I left his side only to shower and sleep. It was in the hospital that I met his mother, Jillian, for the first time. Jillian was a prominent, wealthy Tampa businesswoman. She was always beautiful and impeccably dressed. She was also keenly aware of people. A good judge of character, she was nice but never overly friendly. She saved her opinion about me and her opinion about our relationship until she could further evaluate the situation. By the end of the week, Jillian and I had become friends. She was touched and impressed by my devotion to her son. In all honesty, so was I. Never had I acted so selflessly. Charlie had become the focus of my universe and making him well my full time occupation. Jillian and Charlie had a loving but volatile relationship with much history. Jillian had practically grown up with Charlie, having had him at a young age. Charlie's father had been around for the first few years of Charlie's life. Eventually, he gave into his demons and died a drug addict- in a car accident eerily similar to the one that Charlie would be involved in years later- when Charlie was fifteen. Despite these monumental setbacks, Jillian had built a life for and for her son and had risen to the top of her profession- commercial real estate. She was very successful. She had seen Charlie through diapers, surf trips with teenage buddies, homecoming and prom, his gallery openings, rehab, jail, his accident and all the rest of it. She was a strong and formidable woman with a take no prisoners attitude that applied to her son. She knew all of his bullshit and tolerated none of it. We also bore a striking resemblance to each other which more than one person commented on, including Charlie.

Though our friendship was still in the beginning stages of development, Jillian and I would eventually connect in a way that would be monumental and life changing for both of us. But for now, we just got down to the basics of getting to know each other. I was honest about my work though escorting was something I was not partial to discussing with her. I admitted to having a website which was still taking baby steps but beginning to generate quite an income. She told me about her current project that she was building. We talked about fashion, travel and the arts and discovered that we had quite a lot in common. Charlie watched as we got to know each other, pleased and happy that his mother liked me. Apparently, she had liked very few of his partners in the past. The transsexual issue never came up. I got the feeling she may have suspected or even knew for sure but for us, it was a non-issue. She treated me better than anyone I had ever known. She either liked you or she didn't. If she did, nothing else mattered. She liked me. That was a blessing because with every day that passed, I was falling deeper and deeper in love with Charlie and he with me. When he was released from the hospital, the three of us celebrated with a fabulous dinner at Berns, a very upscale steakhouse in Tampa. It was a perfect evening. Charlie was temporarily free of priapism and I was just happy to have him home. Jillian seemed genuinely happy for both of us. That night we laughed and drank and rejoiced like family. I remember feeling completely happy and carefree and in love. It was an exhilarating moment. But moments are just that, brief passages of time. As always, fate was just around the corner, rearing its ugly little head…Taunting me, yet again.

CHAPTER 56

By the end of that year, Charlie and I were practically living together. He kept a space where he painted and relaxed during the day but at night, home was with me. Meanwhile, my website was beginning to attract national media attention. Suddenly I was the internet "It" girl. I had been so wrapped up in Charlie, I hadn't even noticed. A series of photographs I had posed for had been "hijacked" from my webmaster and had been unleashed on the World Wide Web with amazing ferocity.

The photographs were quickly and without even a second thought to copyright laws, posted to thousands of adult websites and newsgroups across the world. Several hundred straight sites created a special section of interest just to showcase my pictures. Some of the photos were reprinted- once again without permission- in several transsexual sex magazines. These were the kind of magazines that are published once then never seen again which made it nearly impossible to track down the publishers who I most certainly would have sued had I been able to find them. The photos were lush and erotic. In them, I'm wearing a cowboy hat and little else. In print, I was referred to simply as "The Girl in the Hay."

While I plotted legal recourse, the photos grew into a phenomenon. Though my website had begun to generate considerable traffic, no one was prepared for the onslaught of traffic that ensued because of those pictures. Suddenly I began to wonder if the rip off wasn't really a blessing in disguise. I was receiving so many emails a day from fans—at one time over one thousand a day- that the email account attached to my website crashed. I was charging a monthly fee for access to my site and I increased the fee by five dollars. I posted several new pictures and agreed to several layouts in various adult magazines to heighten my exposure. By New Years Eve I was celebrating a tremendous success, having been voted by several online polls "The Most Downloaded Transsexual Model on the Internet." My website was a success, I was in love. Life just couldn't be better. But it's at those precise moments that everything changes.

CHAPTER 57

By February of the following year, Charlie's priapism was be-coming a daily condition and he was relaying heavily on vicodin and oxycontin to control the pain. Though he tried to remain in relatively good spirits regardless of his plight, I noticed a change in him imme-diately. It was harder to make him smile…and he was in a lot of pain and turmoil, emotionally as well as physically. In March, Jillian sent the both of us to The John Hopkins Medical Research Clinic in Bal-timore to seek out the advice of a specialist. He agreed that Charlie's case was one of the most puzzling and severe he had ever seen. By now, Charlie and I were unable to make love on a regular basis and his pe-nis was sore and badly bruised as a result of constantly injecting him-self with neosynephren. His doctor in Tampa was pushing for surgery but was afraid of the outcome. I was at a loss but felt that surgery may be the way out of all this pain. I assured him I would stay with him even if he was rendered impotent and I would have. But he wouldn't hear of it. For a man that had always prided himself on the size of his penis and his considerable prowess in the bedroom, this was a death sentence. By the time we got back to Tampa, the problem was out of control. We were in and out of the emergency room on a daily basis. I had very little time to work on my site or shoot with my photogra-pher who at the time was in Ft. Lauderdale. Without new photos, the traffic was still there but site revenue was suffering. I had to think of something. That's when I turned to what we in the "industry" like to refer to as "cold calls." I had briefly dabbled in "cold calls" after I lost touch with Anthony Lavelle. Cold calls refer to the type of escorting or prostitution that goes on through open advertising. I had met a man in the late nineties that schooled me in the art of "cold calls" and had been quite successful at it. This is how it works.

You place an ad in an adult- based publication. You set up a voice mail to screen the calls. You return the calls and set up a time and place to meet. You charge whatever you feel is appropriate for one hour of your time.

Make no mistake- this was not the glamorous escorting of my Lavelle years. This is not champagne, limos and trips to Europe nor is it rock stars or movie people. This is back to back men- sometimes scheduled no more than fifteen minutes apart. This is mostly professional men but you still get some blue collar guys. Your price usually dictates what kind of man you'll attract. My prices- even for cold calls- was high so I weeded out the riff raff. Cold calls is a cold business. There are countless, nameless men in a day. Every one of them expects you to be a fantasy. Every one of them expects to be treated like the first man of the day. Every one of them wants exactly what they are paying for with no exceptions and no excuses. I was always adept at playing the fantasy. As a result, I built up a regular clientele and within a few months was earning nearly $1500.00 a day. Working again allowed me the financial freedom to spend more and more time with Charlie who was slipping deeper and deeper into despair. Though he didn't approve of my work, he reluctantly accepted it knowing that I knew how to separate love and work as though it were church and state. I always practiced safe sex with my clients and allowed no anal penetration of any kind. Furthermore, I did not offer what is typically referred to as "The GFE" or girl friend experience. I did not allow cuddling, kissing or intimacy of any kind. It was strictly fantasy. My motto was Get Off and Get Out.

So that was my year. Charlie was constantly in and out of the hospitals with brief spurts of wellness here and there. He was by now, addicted to pain meds and became violently ill when his doctor refused to prescribe more pills prior to the required date. Many a night, I would hold his head above the toilet while he vomited, suffering through withdrawal-like symptoms. He would sleep for days at a time recovering. Then he would refill his prescription and it would all start again. It was a vicious cycle and I was much a prisoner of his addiction as he was. As he spiraled further and further out of control, he would disappear to get high with friends, leaving me home, alone and worried. Then he would come back, broken, tired, desperate…and I would take him back again and again and so on and so on until the pattern became routine, even normal. His mother and I were at a loss, unable to do or say anything to get through to him.

"You don't understand what I'm going through…How much pain I'm in," he would scream.

Perhaps we didn't. But we loved him. I couldn't stand to see him destroy himself. His mother refused to put up with it. Tough love, she called it. I tried that. It never worked. I loved him so much I couldn't bear the thought of being without him- not even for a moment. In an attempt to control his addiction, I had nearly forgotten about my own. Though I still went out occasionally and indulged in the recreational line of coke or hit of X, I was pretty much clean at the time. I had to be for him. Eventually, the stress he put on me as well as the exhaustion I was beginning to feel from my work caught up with me. I snapped. After another endless night of partying, Charlie showed up at my door, sick and sad. It took everything in my body- every feeling, every emotion, every ounce of will power, to shut that door in his face. I sank down on the floor and sobbed silently as I listened to him beg me to let him in. His voice was pleading and trembling. Over and over he begged me until there was nothing left for me to hear but the sound of his footsteps walking away and the sound of my own uncontrollable tears.

I refused to take his calls for two weeks. He wrote me letters. They were beautiful and poetic and he expressed his love and his deep regret for the pain he caused me. He wrote that he would win me back. That he would prove himself again. He had checked himself in to the hospital to get better and had begun weaning himself off of the painkillers. He had made up with his mom. He was painting again. All he needed was me, he wrote. I decided that I still needed more time. Even though, I knew in my heart I would take him back, I had to make him wait. I had to show him once and for all, what he was taking for granted. It was important to me that he acknowledge all that I had done. The endless nights of worrying, taking care of him, nursing him back to health, the cross country trips to see doctors and specialists- I wanted him to know that there was only one reason I did and would continue to do it- because I loved him. I loved him with every fiber of my being.

So he waited…and we continued to correspond through cards and letters and eventually through phone calls. He sounded better. He was still in and out of the hospital but for the first time, he was seriously considering the penile surgery. He had had enough, he told me. He had enough pain to last a lifetime. I finally agreed to see him and when they released him from the hospital, I was here to pick him up. For a man with all of his health issues, he was still amazingly good looking. I never got over the sheer magnificence of his physical beauty.

"I want to come home with you," He said once we were in the car.

I thought about it…carefully. There was nothing in the world I wanted more than to have him home with me again. I missed him. I missed everything. But I didn't miss that self destructive streak that enveloped him when the pain kicked in and everything went black. I didn't miss that and I wasn't completely sure that he had kicked it completely.

"Charlie," I said as tenderly as I could, "I want you with me. I love you more than anything in the world. You know what you mean to me. But I cant go back to the way things were."

He cut me off.

"It'll be different," He said, "I promise."

I couldn't say no. Call me crazy in love or just plain crazy but I believed him. I truly believed him.

CHAPTER 58

It wasn't all bad. Really. It wasn't the typical relationship by any means. But it wasn't all bad. There were amazing times together. When I was able to forget about my problems and he was able to forget about his, things could be downright fantastic. Most of you will not be able to comprehend the sheer intensity of our relationship or of any relationship steeped in co dependency. When things were good they were GREAT, when they were bad, they were AWFUL. That is the nature of the beast. He was dealing with health issues and addiction. I was dealing with my own demons, wrestling with my own addictions and HE was quickly becoming the most addictive vice in my life. Taking care of him gave me a sense of worth, a sense of responsibility. Nothing else in my life really had any meaning. Certainly my work had become a problem. A highly paid, highly educated escort is really just a prostitute with a better wardrobe. Even I could admit that to myself. By now, I wasn't even an "escort" any more. I wasn't escorting anyone anywhere. I was an on call three hundred dollar an hour hooker and Charlie was the only thing in my life that offered some sort of refuge from it all. Instead of looking into myself, trying to change myself, I turned all of my energies onto him, fixing him. The good times were my reward but the bad times and helping him through them, my salvation. We would have unforgettable weeks together- shopping, laughing, dancing, traveling. There were romantic dinners and sleepy Sundays on the couch. There was laughter and passion. *THERE WAS LOVE.* That was my happiness. Then came the drugs again and his sickness and his needing me and crying for me in the night. That was my responsibility. And so on and so on until the relationship was messy *AGAIN* and we were both unrecognizable.

***

After Charlie came home, things seesawed for awhile between health and sickness, good and bad, clean and addicted. Eventually, he began to backtrack and before I knew what was happening there we were back at square one. I was at a loss. My friends were pressuring me to leave him once and for all. Lissette loved Charlie but even she was pushing me to come to my senses. But no matter what he did, I couldn't break free. I couldn't let go. My reasoning was that he wasn't hurting me or cheating on me- he was hurting himself. But the more I watched him lose control the more I realized that watching him hurt himself *WAS* hurting me. It was destroying me. One weekend in July, he disappeared. Again. At the same time, Jason called to invite me to celebrate his birthday with several friends at a downtown Tampa nightclub. I explained the situation and he insisted I come. He had always liked Charlie but hated what was happening to him, to us and to me. I reluctantly agreed. The evening was great. There were about fourteen of us and when the club closed, we all went back to a house party that went on well into the next afternoon. I kept checking my cell phone but Charlie didn't call. I took a hit of X and rolled for awhile, trying to forget about Charlie and all of our problems. It didn't work. By the time I came down, I was more miserable than ever. Finally, I gave up and went home. The minute I shut the door behind me, my cell started ringing. I could tell by the number on the caller ID that it was Jillian's cell. I answered quickly. The voice on the other end of the line was not Jillian's.

"Sophia, this is Maxine, Jillian's assistant. I need you to come to Charlie's studio right away."

"Why?" I asked immediately, "Is something wrong?"

Silence.

"Maxine, is something wrong?" I repeated.

After a long pause she spoke.

I remember very little about my initial reaction to her devastating words. I remember dropping the phone and just falling, right there on the floor. I stared straight ahead for what seemed like an eternity. No tears, no movement, just numb. Then I screamed. A horrible, animalistic scream of pain so loud and shocking that my neighbor came to see what was happening.

***

Charlie had died quietly, in his sleep. The love of my life was gone, just like that. There were several factors that contributed to his death but I truly believe, he just gave up and gave out. The police had been called and were at his studio when I arrived. He had been found naked in bed. He was facing the wall. Taped on the wall in front of him, as though it were the last thing he would ever see, was a poster of me. It was the single most devastating moment of my life. Something in me died that day and I have never been able to resuscitate it. *I LOVED HIM. DESPITE THE ISSUES THAT PLAGUED US BOTH, I LOVED HIM. WHATEVER YOUR VIEWS ON ADDICTION, CO DEPENDENCY OR MY LIFE IN GENERAL, YOU MUST BELIEVE THAT. THAT WAS THE ONE TRUTH IN A LIFE FILLED WITH CONFUSION.* Charlie was twenty nine years old when he died.

CHAPTER 59

I had been high for three straight days when the drugs finally stopped working. There is no way to calculate the amount of drugs I consumed but the cocktail of cocaine, ecstasy, GHB and alcohol should have killed me. By the time I realized something was wrong, I was already overdosing. I was in Los Angeles- partying with a very well known Vivid Girl- when it happened. For those of you who aren't familiar, "Vivid Girls" refer to those chosen few adult film stars who are beautiful enough and lucky enough to be put under contract by Vivid Films, the holy grail of porn studio's. I had flown out to Los Angeles at her request and at her expense. We had never met but she was familiar with me from the web and wanted to meet me. She picked me up at LAX and we spent the day hanging out and shopping on Melrose. She was beautiful and sweet and I trusted her. She was pretty straight forward about her attraction to me and about the real reason she had paid for me to come to LA. She had a trick, a very famous Beverly Hills plastic surgeon. He liked to get wild about once a month and wanted me to join them. She promised me ten thousand for three days but said it wouldn't be easy. Three straight days in a suite at The St. Regis. If we wanted food, we ordered it. If we wanted anything, we ordered it. But under no circumstances were we to leave the room until he said so.

"The parties normally last for two or three days, then he falls asleep, pulls himself together and gets back to his life." She told me. "Think your interested?"

At that moment in my life, I could have cared less. I was on a mission. Since burying Charlie two weeks ago with Jillian, I had not been myself. We had flown together to Cleveland and buried him with his grandparents.

Jillian had been strong for me. We had been strong for each other. We had shared a loss that no one could relate to. In an instant, we had both lost the most important person in our lives. She was still in shock and dealing with my devastation had a sobering effect on her. She was all too aware of the pain I was in. What she didn't know was just how far I would go to exterminate it. So I had flown out to LA. To work, party, whatever.

Somewhere in the back of my mind, I must have wanted to die… It was the only explanation for what happened next.

✵✵✵

The St. Regis Beverly Hills is one of the most luxurious hotels in North America. By the time my Vivid Girl and I arrived, our benefactor was already waiting. There was plenty of champagne on ice, lobster and a virtual buffet of fresh fruit and salad waiting for us in the enormous suite he had secured for our "party." When he locked and bolted the door behind us, an enormous feeling of finality gripped me but I shook it off. You can do this I told myself…You can do this! But three straight days with a trick can be an excruciating experience- even with a seasoned pro as your tag team partner. This is how it progressed.

Day One: We get to know each other. Vivid Girl takes the lead. I watch as he fucks her in ever conceivable position. I watch her switch in and out of at least forty different costumes before he finally finds the one that gets him going- again. I watch him choke her. I watch her choke him. I watch her strap on a dildo and fuck him up the ass. I watch him pee on himself and watch as she scolds and disciplines him like a spoiled child.

Day Two: Things start to get a little hairy. Now come the drugs. He smokes crack but doesn't share which is just as well because I don't. Neither does Vivid Girl. But thoughtful guy has made sure to bring along a plethora of pain pills for my curvy friend who squeals in delight when she discovers an endless supply of oxycontin. Just as I'm beginning to feel left out, I find the stash of ecstasy and cocaine and join in the fun. We watch her porn as they continue to fuck and

184

smoke and pop pills. Then it's my turn. He watches as her and I kiss and caress each other and do the usual soundtrack that accompanies these sort of things. I finger her wondering how I got myself into this situation. Then I do another line and it's all okay.

Day Three: Vivid Girl and I are really reaching now. Doing everything we can not to kill him. He's high on crack and crawling around on the floor pretending to be a goat. He's laughing at nothing and acting completely insane. She's done so much oxy I'm surprised she's alive. I've done so many different drugs, I'm beginning to wonder if I'm still alive...or if this is just some kind of weird purgatory complete with beautiful porn star and a crack head plastic surgeon. Now he wants me to suck him which makes me want to throw up. I excuse myself, lock myself in the bathroom and do just that. Next thing I know, crack head is slapping my face and throwing me in an ice cold shower. I can hear faint voices....

Crackhead: "Make her throw up."

Vivid Girl: "I did"

Crackhead: "Stick your finger down her throat."

Vivid Girl is shaking me, trying to get me to open my eyes. She's crying, pleading. Again his annoying voice...

Crackhead: "I think she's coming to...Raquel can you hear me?"

By the time I came around, I was standing in a pool of vomit. Cold water was rushing down on me and for a moment I didn't even know where I was. Vivid Girl and Crackhead heaved a huge sigh of relief. I got myself together and by the time I came out of the bathroom, the party was over. Vivid Girl was collecting our money and Crackhead was cleaning up. Once we were in the car, she handed me the ten grand.

"I'm sorry if I fucked things up," I apologized.

She smiled as she drove toward LAX.

"Don't worry about it sweetie," she said. "If hadn't happened we might still be in that fucking hotel room."

"Besides," she said sweetly as an afterthought, "it isn't a party until someone overdoses."

CHAPTER 60

I had a problem. I had a big problem. I just didn't realize it because, unlike your average addict, I was making so much money that my lifestyle never suffered on account of my addiction- nor, miraculously, did my looks. I had everything I wanted. A beautiful apartment, a brand new BMW, the finest clothes, shoes and bags that money could buy. What I didn't have was Charlie...and it was killing me. My life, nearly one year after his death, had degenerated into an endless succession of late nights in clubs on both coasts and everywhere in between. New York, South Beach, Las Vegas, Los Angeles, Seattle, Boston, Dallas, Key West, New Orleans and of course, Tampa. Tampa was always the cruelest of my mistresses- The one who fucked me up the most and spit me out the quickest. I should have left but her hold was tight and unrelenting. I saw clients during the day and sometimes well into the evening. The money was a constant. I had the freedom and financial capability to live as I wanted to. At midnight, I would hit the clubs, all the clubs. Gay or straight, it didn't matter. I had fans in both. I would snort coke all night every night- sometimes with friends, sometimes with the guys I'd pick up in the bars. I was a star in Tampa and every club owner in town wanted me at their table. Everyone from bartenders to management to valet knew me at every hotspot in town and they knew to take care of me. Drugs were free most of the time, cheap when they weren't. The hottest guys in town were mine for the asking. If I saw two guys I liked and couldn't decide which one I wanted, I'd take them both...sometimes there were three or four of them at a time. The less intimacy, the better. They never refused. I pushed the envelope. Forcing straight men into bisexual situations with each other became my favorite pastime. I was always surprised at how far they would go. After awhile, it stopped surprising me and it stopped amusing me. And of course there were always, the women. The beautiful strippers and escorts who pursued me shamelessly until I finally gave in.

It was a time of unparalleled sex in my life. However, my perception of what constitutes good sex differs strongly from most peoples. I have never enjoyed being penetrated by anyone other than someone I have deep feelings for, no pun intended. So as a result, I never engaged in anything more than extensive oral sex with any of the men or women I picked up. As my wild life spiraled out of control, my legend in Tampa grew. The nationally syndicated host of the much listened to "Bubba The Love Sponge" morning show on The Clear Channel Network had "discovered" my website and was publicizing it loud and clear for the world to hear. Listeners were calling into share their stories and sightings as though I were some sort of unexplained occurrence like UFO's or Bigfoot. By this time, my image on the internet had reached iconic proportions. My photographs were being shot by some of the country's top photographers and I was appearing on adult magazine covers across the country. I was the first and only transsexual to appear on the cover of Tampa's V2 Magazine- a widely read, heavily circulated straight publication catering to Tampa's adult entertainment industry. There was such a huge response to my first cover that a second one quickly followed.

Those covers led to a meeting with one of the most famous rock stars on the planet who found an issue backstage at The Ice Palace where he had just performed with his band. What surprised me was that he just called me directly. No manager, no roadie, just flat out called me and asked for a meeting. I didn't believe it was him. I almost didn't go. I'm glad I did. It was a memorable meeting fueled by massive amounts of cocaine. I saw him again in Lauderdale and when I flew out to LA a month later, we got together again. By the time I met up with him again on The Lollapalooza Tour, I think he had tired of his walk on the wild side. He wasn't performing at the festival and he just kept walking around in a huff complaining about how commercial it had all become. He was being rude and arrogant to everyone around him including his fans and me. There were several other up and coming stars who were trying to connect with him, show their love but he was just downright distant. He was also snorting a lot of heroin and I didn't really want any part of that scene. To tell you the truth, he wasn't really my type. I guess the groupie in me just kicked in and wanted to fuck a rock star. Eventually, I got bored with hanging around waiting for his personality to kick in and wandered off into the masses. But that backstage pass at Lollapalooza came in quite handy. And he wasn't the only rocker who rocked my world that weekend. There were porn stars everywhere and playmates and girlfriends and wives. Competition was fierce and getting noticed and hooking up with someone you wanted or wanted you, next to impossible. But, as always, I got the one I wanted. He was in one of the smaller bands but so hot nonetheless. There were a few girls around him but he found his way over easily enough. We didn't say a whole lot but it sure was a good time. I don't remember much about the music though.

By the time I returned to Tampa, my sexscapades were becoming the stuff of legend. I was routinely seen cavorting in nightclubs with high profile athletes who did their best to keep their attraction to me a secret. One night I left The Hyde Park Café with two Yankee players who were in town for spring training and believe me, they knew. And they loved it. There was the Baltimore Raven. The pro NBA player. There were the lawyers, plastic surgeons and everyone in between including most of Tampa's hottest male dancers. Many of them were flings, some wanted more but in the end, I chose to be alone. I've always been a loner. Another problem I had with dating a high profile man was their inability to accept WHAT I WAS. I had long moved past the men who wanted to keep the relationship our little secret. If a man isn't man enough to be with the person he wants to be with, I just move on.

My experience with them and with one Tampa athlete in particular, left a lot to be desired in more ways than one. Most are complete egomaniacs. The world has to revolve, at all times, around them. And by now you must know that I was way too self absorbed to put up with any of that bullshit. But it was fun while it lasted and when I run into them now as I occasionally do, they give me a wink and that all knowing smile. The one that says, *YOU BEAUTIFUL, SCANDALOUS BITCH, I CANT STOP THINKING ABOUT YOU!*

CHAPTER 61

I had pulled myself out of bed to make it to the hair salon. It was Saturday afternoon and though I had only had about two hours sleep, I knew I had to keep the appointment. I had front row tickets and a backstage pass to the Sugar Ray concert and I wasn't going to miss it for anything.

I was going with Liza. Liza, you may remember, was the colorful, wildly beautiful diva whom I'd first met through Ricky years ago in Key West. I had reconnected with her through Charlie during the course of our relationship. She and I had become increasingly close since his death. She had been extremely supportive, taking me off to her beautiful Key West compound to heal and get my head together after the LA incident. She was to become a very special person in my life. We had much in common. A love of fashion, travel, entertainment and of course, cocaine. I had finally found my fellow thrill seeker and believe me she could outmatch me drink for drink, bump for bump.

***

The concert was hot. Uncle Kracker opened and rocked the house. We had front row seats and a succession of bands played before the very gorgeous Mark McGrath finally took the stage. Needless to say, I looked hot and was dancing out front doing my best to get him to notice me. It didn't work. Backstage was no better as he was surrounded by tons of people. Of course, the drummer from this band and the bass player from the other band and the front man of so and so were all quick to pounce on me. But I wanted Mark. Liza, who was in the throes of a passionate love affair with a former Tampa Bay Buccaneer, insisted on leaving early to get back to him. I left with her but promised one of the bass players I would meet up with him later. After picking up my car from Liza's place, I hightailed it to The Hideaway. The Hideaway was a Tampa hotspot owned by my friend Corey. It was also a pretty popular place to catch visiting musicians. My bass player was already there with several other guys from the various bands but alas, no Mark. So I toyed with the bass player for awhile who was desperately trying to get me into the bathroom. But my heart was set on Mark so after a little heavy petting, I left the bass player there and moved on to the next club and on to the next kick. I went off to Twilight in Ybor City and that's where I first met Beth.

✼✼✼

The hair salon of the moment was a South Tampa studio called Bella Donna. Anyone who was anyone and even the nobody's that thought they were somebody went out of their way to guarantee an appointment with one of the many talented stylists. It was a stone's throw from my apartment and there were several stylists on call who were guaranteed to fit me in, no matter what time of the day and regardless of how busy they were. My old friend Hector was there. My favorite stylist, John, was always available. There was David, another old friend. There was Drew, a so hot heavily tattooed stylist and guitarist with a formally famous punk rock band. And of course, there was David's girlfriend Beth.

Beth became to me that summer of 2003 what Sierra had been years earlier. One of those rare female infatuations. She was very striking and similar to Sierra in so many ways. She was tall and thin with a perfect body complete with the prerequisite DD implants. Her face was beautiful with high cheekbones and soft lips. She was also keenly aware of her effect on men which I found immensely attractive. But perhaps, most important of all, she was completely in awe of me which of course demonstrated remarkably good taste. She was a hairdresser by day, stripper by night and although she pursued me quite boldly for awhile, it was a full two months before I finally gave in to her. My harmless crush on Drew had turned into an out and out flirtation and one night, after much drinking and endless amounts of cocaine and crystal meth, I found myself in bed with not only him but Beth and David as well. After much frolicking with the boys, Beth and I turned our attention on each other. It was intimate, as though they weren't even there, even if the sound of David jacking off to our display was a bit loud. She was an amazing kisser. I found myself experiencing something quite different. Something real. And I liked it. Sex with men had always been hot and heady. I enjoyed their strength and masculinity and the roughness that came with their forceful nature. But with Beth, I found a softness that I had been lacking. I found myself wanting to please her sensuously- not sexually. It was the beginning of an incredible summer with one of the hottest human beings I've ever known.

***

There is no doubt in my mind that what I found with Beth was the closest thing to sexual intimacy and feeling that I have ever experienced with a female. She was involved in a very volatile relationship with David and though our friendship excited him to no end, it also caused him much grief and more than one sleepless night. She and I reveled in the scandal that we were causing. We were the premier party girls and every man was dying to get between us and a couple did. But for the most part, it was just us and David when they weren't fighting. The drugs of course, were still there. But they took a back seat to our all out pursuit of pleasure. It was, even for me, a sexually liberating experience. You see, sex had become a tool for me. A way to make money, control someone or reinforce my deep seated need for acceptance. It had been a long time since I had just given myself up to it and enjoyed it for the sheer fun of it. The fact that I was able to rediscover that with a WOMAN made it even more extraordinary. It was an exciting time. Later, when we posed together for my website, the black and white images that emerged remain some of the most sensuous of my career. It was refreshing to be surprised—to find that even a jaded soul such as mine could find release and freedom in the one place I never thought to search. She opened my eyes to the secret pleasures of the feminine mystique. Eventually, as all things do, our infatuation ran its course. And though I am always on the look out for that next special girl (believe me they are rare) Beth remains the last woman in my life and a very good friend to this day.

CHAPTER 62

In late 2003, I decided to go into rehab. It was one of the most difficult decisions I have ever had to make. But I knew that if I didn't, I would die. .. Or worse, I would continue to wake up every morning with *That Feeling*. And anyone who has been there knows that *That Feeling* is worse than anything else in the world. It is a feeling that is devoid of any real feeling at all and that is the strangest feeling of all- it's an emptiness, a nothingness that envelops you and the world becomes a very lonely place when your caught up in it. I cant tell you how many times I woke up with *That Feeling* or couldn't get to sleep because I had done too much coke and had too suffer through That Feeling until my body finally shut down and I slept. I was no longer doing drugs. The drugs, as they say, were doing me. No matter how much money I made, what I drove, where I lived or what I wore, the song remained the same- I was a junkie. Drugs had become an emotional as well as a physical outlet for me. An escape. I had been, by this time, escaping for years. I decided as I neared yet another birthday, that the time for running was over. I would now have to face what I had been running from all along. Myself. Would I be ready to do that? I wasn't sure. What I knew was that I was going to try and that was more than I had ever been willing to do and that, they say, is the first step.

The night before I went into rehab, I went out. I called several friends, all of whom knew nothing of my plans, and proceeded to throw myself a secret bon voyage party. I went club hopping and ended up back at my place around midnight which was so early for me. I was high, drunk and lonely. I decided to call someone I had just recently met. His name was James and for the first time in a long time, I had met a man that I was completely and utterly attracted to. No money, no agenda- just wild, animalistic, mind-blowing sex. He was in his late thirties, with beautiful blue eyes that I was immediately fond of. He had a nice tight swimmers build and his considerable endowment beneath the buckle was more than enough to satisfy my size obsession. He lived about an hour from me but was more than willing to drive over. I waited patiently for him. Rehab was just hours away but I was determined to go out with a bang. When he arrived, we went right at it. He had barely made it through the door before I had his shirt off. We started in the living room, continued on the stairs and ended on the second floor of my apartment which was actually just one large bedroom with an amazing view of Downtown Tampa. We were soaked in sweat by the time it was over.

He was, to put it simply, an amazing fuck. Exactly what I needed. I picked up the phone and called my sister to let her know that I was going into rehab the next morning. She was concerned. In a tearful twenty minute conversation I explained why I was doing it, completely forgetting the fact that Jim was still in bed with me and privy to more information than I would have liked him to have about me. When I hung up, I still had tears in my eyes. Jim moved closer to me.

"Don't feel sorry for me," I said as he pulled me toward him.

"I don't," he said simply.

"Will you stay with me tonight...just till I fall asleep?" I asked him.

"I will stay with you the whole night," he replied.

And just like that- for the first time since Charlie- I felt completely at ease in a man's arms and allowed myself to fall asleep.

CHAPTER 63

The most important thing that any one contemplating volun-
tary rehab should know is that:
*IT ONLY WORKS IF YOU WANT IT TO. IT ONLY WORKS IF
YOUR WILLING TO CHANGE.*
The rehab I chose was far from Tampa. It wasn't a state or feder-
ally funded program. I spent several thousand dollars for a top of the
line place and it did not get me off drugs but it did open my eyes to a
lot of what was going on inside my head. I had taken every precaution
to make sure I chose a place that could not forcibly keep me once I
was inside. I wanted to be able to come and go at will. That sense of
freedom was very important to me. The thought of being locked up
like my father was something I just couldn't bear. So two days into
my therapy, I left. Then I came back...and left again. By the time I
returned, I was in desperate need of guidance.

I didn't know what to do or who to turn to. I had come to the
full realization that my addiction had me, quite literally, by the balls.
The drugs scared me, no doubt about it. But what frightened me most
was the prospect of life- WITHOUT THE DRUGS. Not because I
would miss the high or would have to give up half if not most of my
friends. But because- for the first time in a decade- I would have to
face life- my life and all the choices I had made and all of the people
I had fucked and loved and lost- and I would have to face it knowing
full on that at the end of that hard long look at myself, there would be
no silver lining to my dark cloud. There would be no line of cocaine
or hit of X. Because if I do this I promised myself, I will do this right.
I have always prided myself on being a very strong person. I have sur-
vived as a transsexual in a very cruel world and I have, regardless of
how I had to do it, done it on my own with very little help or no help
at all from family or friends.

I have lost very important people in my life- my mother, my father, my lover…And gone on by pushing it away, not thinking about it, forgetting it ever happened, forgetting, in a sense, that I ever loved them at all. That is how I managed. And the drugs helped. They did. They were my allies. They helped me forget and that's why I needed them. They were my family. My surrogate family. I spent two days with a therapist discussing, in length, my life. She was amazed that I had made it this far. She said that considering the hand that life had dealt me she found my ability to adapt to the world at large "quite impressive." She also told me that if I wasn't ready to take control of my life- right then and there- I was wasting my time and my money and that I should just leave. And that's what I did. I decided to leave rehab knowing full well that I hadn't learned a thing…except for one very important thing that the therapist told me as I was leaving. She said:

"You know Sophia, your entire life has been about acceptance and payback. Paying back the ones who hurt you when you were a boy. You so believed what they said about you- the horrible things they said- that you had to become someone else to be happy. I'm surprised that you have adapted to the change as well as you have. You don't seem to have any problem living as a woman. You make a very beautiful one. But you just seem to have a problem living with yourself. The inside is all that counts. Because you are still the same person. No matter what you do to the outside, you are still that scared little boy inside. You've seen a bit of the world, you've developed some thick skin. You've loved. You are lucky. Some of us never love. But your wasting away and one day your going to wake up and all that beauty is going to be gone…and your going to just die wondering how you spent so much time and money and effort working on the outside and never getting around to the inside. You have at least a few good people in your life that see and love the goodness in you. Why can't you see that in yourself?"

The tears were falling silently down my face as she left me standing in the hallway, alone and disappointed. I packed my bags and left that day. It was an attempt at soul searching that may not have worked at the time. But it was a breakthrough of sorts. For the first time, I knew that it was wrong. All of it was wrong. My life, my choices, but more than anything, the running...the drugs. This shot at rehab may have failed. But next time would be different, I promised myself, next time will be different.

CHAPTER 64

By the time I got back to Tampa, I had come to terms with my life. I knew that if I was ever going to live a somewhat normal existence, I had to make some changes. First, I would begin the painful inward journey of self analysis. I would take everything in stages and deal with them accordingly. I was determined to deal with each death, each choice, each addiction. Then I would accept them, file them away as a lesson learned, and move on. More importantly, I was going to do this on my own. It wasn't that I didn't have faith in therapy. I did. But a therapist's role isn't quite as complex as people think. A therapist points out what you already know about yourself but are afraid to see. It's their job to illuminate you- to show you the things you can't see clearly or ignore altogether and to work toward a solution that will allow you a better chance at happiness. They don't offer a fool proof method. *Only YOU can cure YOU.*

So with all the chutzpah I could muster, I began taking baby steps to change my life. I gave myself one last year to get it together. After that, there would be no more excuses. My attempts at self analysis moved slowly. I began with my first memory of childhood. Eating ice cream in the snow with my mother and my sister. Then I moved on to other images. They came to me in flashes. My father being arrested. My mother screaming to the police officers "Not in front of my children." Then happy times. Just me and mom and Josette. Not a lot of money, but happy times. I realized, early on, that a lot of my pain in childhood had been derived from peers. Being from Tampa and having continued to spend time there well into adulthood, I had been afforded the unique opportunity of seeing these peers throughout the years. The boys that had chased me home from school. The ones who called me a fag, a sissy. The ones who said and did countless horrible things to me all in the name of fun. And dealing with this particular painful memory was considerably easier than I thought. You see, I had already extracted my revenge. I had systematically sought out every single one of them. The high school jocks, the "cool crowd". They weren't hard to find. Guys like that never make it far. And you know what? They had a whole different opinion of me, years later, down on their knees. So even though this journey of self discovery wasn't supposed to be about revenge, those boys were one exception to the rule. Now when I think about my childhood and the ones that made it miserable, I have a whole different perspective. Kids will be kids. They can be cruel. But let this be a cautionary tale for all those macho little men out there. The next time you see an effeminate boy on the playground, tread carefully- you may end up sucking his dick later.

I then began to explore my volatile relationship with my step father who at the time was still alive and living in the house I grew up in. I had hated him for years. I loathed the fact that he was living in a house that my mother had worked most of her adult life to pay for. A home that she had wanted my sister and I to have. But I knew that it was God's will. He was old and alone in that house. Blind and sick and half crazy. He was being punished in ways I could never imagine. It must have been hard for this self sufficient man to watch himself rot away- without a friend or family member in sight. He died- alone- in the house that was never a home. My sister and I did eventually take control of the property and bull dozed it to the ground. It was invigorating. But the truth is, I had moved past him long ago, and though I secretly wished him a painful death, when my sister called me in Key West to tell me that he had died, I felt nothing. No sadness, no happiness. Just absolutely nothing.

Next up, my mother. I drove out to the cemetery where she was buried. I spent the day talking to her. I cut fresh flowers and placed them in her vase. I kissed her crypt and told her that I probably wouldn't be back but that I would always love her and that she would always be a part of my soul. Now when I think of my mother, I don't think of the bad stuff. I remember the good times. I remember her laughter and her zest for life. I remember how she took care of us when we were little. How strong she was. I am proud to be her child.

I miss her terribly. I still dream about her. I love dreaming about her. That's the wonderful things about dreams. You always get to revisit the ones you love. And the ones you've lost.

Analyzing my relationship, or lack thereof, with my father was particularly hard. If only he'd been there. I finally realized that he had been. Not in the conventional way. But my father had, from behind bars, always made an attempt to remain in contact with me. He wrote letters, he called when he could. I was the one that walked away. Twenty five years is a long time to wait for someone. I didn't have the patience. I am thankful that in the end, we did find each other again. And when he died, I held his hand. I was there too to scatter his ashes at sea as he had requested. More than anything, I'm thankful that those last several months and especially those few precious moments toward the end were spent outside. You see, I had never been able to see my father anywhere except in prison. And even though, I couldn't give myself up to him completely when he got out, I gave what I could and he understood and he loved me in spite of everything. I look like my father. I see him in my face. And I like that.

And Charlie. My Charlie. The first one I loved, truly loved. Just gone. How bitter I was. Always blaming myself or him or both of us. But I don't. I don't anymore. Sometimes it's hard to understand how I managed to love him at all. He was, like me, so complex. But isn't that what makes us who we are? It's the good AND the bad. People often forget that. It's all of our rich complexities that make us so memorable, so unforgettable, so absolutely irresistible. I always told him, "I love you for you but I wish I could change the bad stuff," to which he would reply, "I just love you." That was Charlie. He loved me in spite of my issues which were considerable. He never tried to change me. And isn't that what love-real love- is all about? I look back and know that there was a reason that he had drifted in and out of my life for so long. It was all a build up. It was a precursor to what came later. He needed someone to love and care for him at the end of his life. I needed to know that I was capable of unconditional love. How fortunate that we found each other. I miss him every day but it gets easier every day. He would want me to move on. And I have. But still, there is a moment in every day when my heart calls out to him. I'm afraid that may always be the case. There are some people you never forget. He is one of them.

***

And what about, most importantly, the loss of myself? Because I did lose myself some where along the way and it hasn't been easy trying to find myself again. Do I regret becoming a woman? Do I regret the choices I made? Do I regret the drugs, the tricking? I guess I could. But I don't. I am unabashedly unapologetic about the choices that I made in my life, knowing full well that the only person they ever truly affected were me. I was a good son/daughter to my mother, a good brother/sister to my sister, an unconditional lover and caregiver to Charlie and a true and generous friend to every friend in my life. I gave more of myself than most people are required to. So I should be ashamed of the fact that I changed my sex? That it's perceived by some as deceiving and treacherous? I have never been embarrassed of my sex or lack thereof. If anyone asks, I am honest about my gender status. The fact that they never ask, that they never even seem to suspect, at the gym, in the mall, in a restaurant, only proves to me that this is the way it was supposed to be. As far as the religious repercussions, don't even get me started on that. I am a spiritual person. But my belief in a higher power does not include confessing my sins to a priest or singing in a church choir. I believe that people should worship however they choose. When I need to be near God, I walk on a beach or just speak to Him from my heart, no matter where I am. I am a good person, in spite of all this, and *I KNOW HE HEAR'S ME*. As far as my gender status, I am as of this writing, a pre-operative transsexual. I look, sound, feel, live as a woman but I am not a woman, not fully. Even if I had my final surgery, would that make me a woman? Again, the answer is no, not clinically, not technically. For me, Woman, Female, is what exists inside of my head and inside of my heart, inside of my soul. I have the soul of a woman. For me, that has always been enough. Looking like a beautiful woman and having a penis has never been, believe it or not, a hindrance. Funny, isn't it? What is perceived by the majority of society as freakish or unnatural is the very thing that has allowed me to see the world and live in luxury most of my adult life. When the day comes that I finally decide that I WANT to be complete physically, I am fortunate enough to know one of the leading specialists in the field. He is my dear friend and he has assured me that when I am ready. . .

CHAPTER 65

Life was becoming easier. My drug binges were a thing of the past. I had, finally, put some of my demons to rest. When those rare moments of melancholy embraced me, I put on some music, opened up my photo albums and revisited the friends and family I'd lost. I also began spending more and more time with Jillian, Charlie's mother, who as it turned out, was quickly becoming a sister to me. We traveled constantly- Puerto Rico, shopping trips to New York City. She was a warm and wonderful influence on me. I found the kind of good, clean fun that I was looking for and before I knew what was happening, drugs were becoming less important to me. I had also made a wonderful new friend named Christine. She was a beautiful dancer and former addict who had cleaned up her act. She had kicked her habits alone and without professional assistance. She always believed I could and would change. She never pressured me but she was always there to listen and to offer advice. She was instrumental in my wanting to change. She inspired me and continues to do so to this day.

And then there was Jim. Somehow before I knew what was happening, I found myself falling in love with the kindest man I'd ever known. Ever since that night he held me in his arms- the night before I checked into rehab- I had been unable to shake the thought of him. We had continued to see each other- off an on- for several months but I was unwilling to commit to anything more than a sexual relationship. I know now as I did then that the reason for my reluctance was because I knew with the utmost certainty that I could fall in love with him and I was scared of love and scared of being hurt again.

But in keeping step with my new outlook on life, I finally agreed to dinner and drinks. Dinner and drinks was a huge step for me. I'm sure your wondering why this was such a difficult step to make considering the fact that I had been to bed with the man several times.

But to me, with very few exceptions, sex had never been about intimacy. It had been about physical gratification and power. Sex in my mind was easier than dinner. Dinner required conversation, getting to know each other. All I really knew about Jim was that he was one of the most passionate, sexual human beings I had ever known and I was extremely attracted to him. I had met him in a straight club in Ybor. He was with someone I knew and I noticed him checking me out. He was very confident in a quiet way which I really liked. When he struck up a conversation, I cut to the chase as I tended to do when I was high and horny. I was honest with him about my gender status and asked him if he wanted to go back to my place. He readily agreed. Though he had never been with someone like me, he was curious. The fact that he was man enough to admit that to me and to himself was a huge turn on. Our sexual relationship had progressed from there. Now, nearly one year after having sex with him on countless occasions, I was going to have my first meal with him. We went to a casual place for dinner and then went to Shangri-La for drinks. Shangri-La was an upscale bikini bar that I had frequented over the years. The owners and management knew me well. We took a seat in the VIP section, far from the madness of the ghetto fabulous crowd that the bar tended to attract. Jim said very little. He listened mostly. I carefully watched his eyes, hoping to catch him checking out the other girls.

He didn't. In fact, he didn't take his eyes off me. Later that night, back at my place, for the first time since Charlie died, I allowed myself to kiss- really kiss- another man. We made out for hours. Deep, passionate kissing that seemed to go on and on. By the time we stopped kissing, it was early morning and the sun was coming up. We feel asleep, not having had sex. This time, we had made love...and it was strange...And wonderful.

***

Jim became a constant in my life and the more and more time we spent together, the more I grew to care for him. To understand him is to know him. He is the most laid back individual I have ever known. He has never been into drugs or partying and always did what he could to deter me from that lifestyle though he never tried to control me. When he finally told me he loved me, I knew I felt the same way. What we were going to do about it was another thing entirely. Jim had a fifteen year old daughter and wasn't quite sure how to tell her. He had a wonderful relationship with her and insisted upon total honesty. That was another admirable quality that convinced me that this was a good man, a true man. He was also hardworking, dependable and gorgeous and even I know you don't find a man like that every day. He went through a lot of soul searching for several months. I could see how difficult it was for him. I had become so accustomed to my life and my way of life that I had almost forgotten that what I perceive as normal may not be seen that way by most people. There was a struggle going on inside of him. He loved me and I loved him. But it wasn't that simple. One night he broke down and crying, he told me he just didn't think he could do it. He just didn't think he had it in him to deal with his family, his friends. He just couldn't do it. I held him and told him understood. The funny thing was- I did understand. I totally understood. So we went on.. Until it became unbearable for me and I finally told him I couldn't see him anymore. If he wasn't capable of giving himself to me completely, come what may, I had to go. He thought about it for a long time and admitted that he didn't think he was. It wasn't a break up. It was an understanding. I knew I was in love. But you know the old saying, Let it go, if it comes back...So, I let go and rather than go out and get fucked up over it, I got in my car and drove. I didn't know for sure where I was going. What I did know for sure was that my time in Tampa had come to an end.

CHAPTER 66

I ended up in Savannah, GA. Savannah had always been a very special place for me. I had visited several times over the years, with Lissette, alone. It is a hauntingly beautiful place and unlike anywhere else in the world. One has the feeling of being transported in time while walking through its charming, historic streets and moss-covered parks and cemeteries. I decided to lose myself there for awhile. I spent a long weekend at The President's Quarters. I went shopping on River Street. I had dinner at The Olde Pink House. It was a particularly beautiful day in Savannah when I found myself at the door of one of the larger real estate companies in town. When I left the office half an hour later, I had a list of properties in my hand. I wasn't sure what I was going to do with them but I had already made up my mind that I was leaving Tampa and Savannah would be my new home.

I looked at over twenty different properties. I finally settled on an apartment in the historic district that was vaguely reminiscent of a place I had rented on Davis Island. With complete assurance that the place would be renovated and ready by the time I reached Savannah on October 1, 2004 I wrote out a check for three thousand dollars and headed back home to pack my stuff. I had a little over a month to get myself ready and say my goodbye to Tampa. But first, there was Argentina.

CHAPTER 67

I left for Buenos Aries on September 1, 2004 exactly one month before I had to be in Savannah. I went with Liza and it was a memorable trip all things considered. It was a week of little sleep, great food, great company and lots of champagne. We partied till dawn in the streets of Buenos Aries. The city was exciting and rich with life and drama. There was a bit of political unrest so it wasn't unusual to find riot police and political protesters just steps from our hotel lobby. It was a city filled with beautiful men and women. It was an experience I'll never forget. Liza and I had a blast. By the time I got back to Florida, it was time for me to start packing. I also knew that it was time to say goodbye to several of my "friends" and that was okay too. I made it a point to see everyone one last time, including Jim.

Saying goodbye to Jim wasn't easy. There were a lot of tears on both sides. Why did love have to be so hard? We convinced each other that it was for the best though I'm not sure either of us believed it. He insisted upon accompanying me to Savannah just to make sure I got "settled in alright". Even when I protested, assuring him the movers could handle it, he still insisted on coming. So on the first of October he tailgated me all the way to Savannah. It was a bittersweet arrival in my new home. Savannah was just as I left it. Unfortunately, so was the apartment. No renovation had been done. In fact, it was worse than before. I immediately contacted the owner of the building who as it turned out lived in Rhode Island and had no idea what was going on. I was, to say the least, completely irate. I demanded the return of my money and told her the deal was off. She didn't dispute it when I told her that as far as I was concerned, she was in breach of contract. I further advised her that I was taking photographs of the property and unless I had my money within one week, my attorney would seek legal action. She agreed and promptly hung up on me. Then I called my movers who, thank God, had not left Tampa and instructed them to store my items. Then I fell into Jim's arms and cried.

"I cant believe this is happening," I said.

"This isn't the way it's supposed to be Sophia," he replied. "Your supposed to be with me."

"I cant go back to Tampa," I told him.

"Then don't. We don't have to be in Tampa. But I want to be with you. I'm ready to make that commitment. This only proves that Savannah is not where you belong."

I thought about it. Life had always had a funny way of looking out for me. It had, on many occasions, saved me, in spite of the foolish decisions I often made. Maybe he was right. Maybe this just wasn't the place for me. I told him I would have to think about it before I made any rash decisions. He agreed that was best. We made the most of Savannah by staying the weekend. It was wonderful to be in that beautiful place with him. Even the outcome of my move had done nothing to hamper my enthusiasm or love of the place. I took him to all of my favorite spots and we drove to Tybee Island and watched the sunset. We stayed at The Presidents Quarters and made quiet love well into the early morning. By the time we set out for Florida, I was disappointed but sure that was waiting for me with him was better than anything I could have done on my own in Savannah.

CHAPTER 68

And so it was with much trepidation but with the best intentions that I temporarily returned to Tampa. I moved into Jillian's beautiful estate on Bayshore Blvd and began a chapter in my life of unparalleled happiness. My time with Jillian was wonderful. The house was a haven for me. A sanctuary that allowed me the opportunity to truly begin the completion of this book which has been a constant struggle for me. After two years of making notes and jotting down remembrances, I finally began the painstaking task of putting it into written form. And it just flowed. It was exhilarating, terrifying, sad, and liberating. It was the single most important step in my recovery and in finding some sort of inner peace. I realized early on that I couldn't include everything or everyone that had touched my life. This is the stuff that came to me, the stuff that mattered, the stuff I had to put down and put away. So in that beautiful house on the water, I wrote and read and enjoyed fabulous home cooked meals with two people in my life that truly mattered- Jillian...and Jim. Jillian, as any true friend would be, was ecstatic that I had found love again. It didn't matter that Charlie had been her son. I was her friend. Charlie was gone. It was touching to see how she took to Jim and opened her heart and her home to this simply wonderful man. My relationship with him just grew and grew. It was as if I had known him all of my life. He was still living over an hour away from Tampa but without fail, he went to work everyday and if he didn't drive to Tampa in the evenings, I would drive to him. We had begun to discuss the idea of living together. I had met his mother and his daughter and his brother. There were no more secrets, no more lies. It was the happiest time in my life. It seems ironic though highly understandable given my life history that something unexpected should happen. A monkey wrench. One more thing to fuck with me, if just a little.

It's highly confusing to me that during the most sober period in my life I was stopped, detained and arrested for Suspicion of DUI. The sad part is that I was actually driving someone home who had attempted to drive while under the influence. When the officer pulled me over, I admitted to having two drinks at dinner which was the absolute truth. I had no alcohol or drugs in my car or on my person. I spoke clearly to the officer and answered all of his questions promptly. I offered to leave my car and use my cell phone to call a cab. He suggested I take a DUI test, which I refused to do. I became more and more angry as he ran my drivers license, convinced that I was being harassed. I have never been arrested in my life, believe it or not. I had no outstanding or unpaid tickets. I hadn't even been pulled over in nearly three years. But still, the officer persisted. I allowed him to search my car. Nothing. I allowed him to search me. Nothing. When I informed him that I was a transsexual, things really got good. Suddenly, I either had to submit to the DUI tests or I was going to jail. I took a long look at the officer, asked him to secure my Jaguar and placed my hands behind my back. I wasn't going to play this game. I decided then and there that I was going to jail and that my attorney could deal with it later.

The officer wasn't happy about my reluctance to cooperate. He handcuffed me, put me in the patrol car and off I went to The Orient Road Holding Facility, just outside of Tampa. There I stayed for eight hours. I bailed out, went home and went to sleep. The next morning my attorney requested a copy of the video tape that was shot from the patrol car at the time of my arrest. Two months later, The Department Of Motor Vehicles reinstated my license because they felt there wasn't sufficient evidence to support a charge of DUI. Funny how things work out. I drive around under the influence for years. The one time I'm sober and my life's on track, I'm charged with DUI. But that's how it goes. In the end, it all worked out.

CHAPTER 69

I left Jillian's place shortly before my birthday in November of 2004. Even the drama of my arrest had done nothing to dampen my spirits. I was happy and in love. I had removed myself from the lure of drugs and the people who had, for years, helped facilitate my abuse. I left Tampa for good to be with Jim. We moved into a beautiful home in The Keys and gradually, with his help, I truly began to heal. Our home became an ideal place to build a love—a bastion of peace, tranquility and a happiness I had never really experienced before. In that home, on that beautiful island, we spent days relaxing in the sun, sharing our dreams, our feelings, our thoughts. We danced and laughed and made love. We entertained friends and family. With his help, I rediscovered the person I was—before the drugs, the nightlife, the self destruction had taken their toll. With his help, I came to realize that the best party in the whole world can be right in your very home—surrounded by the books, the art and the people that you love the most. I began spending quality time with my nephews, my sister, Jillian and Lissette. In the summer of 2005, Jim and I traveled to Peru and it was a life changing experience. We spent two weeks traveling through this amazing country—high on the culture, the people, the very essence of life that permeated everything we saw, touched, felt. We spent two days in the fabled lost city of Macchu Picchu. I have seen many places in my life but nothing prepared me for the splendor and the breathtaking beauty of this spiritual place. We did reach the top of the summit. It is an exhausting and physically draining climb of several thousand feet that many do not or cannot make. But we did. Together. By the time we reached the top we were literally above the clouds and seemingly, at the very edge of the earth. As we sat there quietly, drinking in the amazing view, I suddenly realized that I had been clean for nearly a year. That I was sitting, happily and sober at one of the most spectacular places on earth with a man I loved and I felt higher than I ever had. It was a life changing experience. At that moment, I realized LIFE IS BEAUTIFUL. You have to live your dreams everyday. Every moment has to count. Every place, every person whose life you touch or those who touch you—IT MATTERS. FEELING MATTERS. The Good and the bad. You have to feel it all. Embrace it and understand it and keep moving on. Jim helped me understand that most of all. He is an amazing man with a tremendous amount of love and feeling. Our relationship did eventually run its course. There was no big break up. No drama. Just a mutual understanding that although we loved and cared for each other, we both wanted different things from life. I am artistic and I love beautiful things. He is an athlete who enjoys surfing, kite boarding, base jumping and snowboarding. But our experience together was one of the most rewarding experiences of my life. He armed me with the tools to move on to the next phase of my life. He helped me be a better, stronger person and for that I will always be grateful.

***

After my relationship ended with Jim, my life took some interesting turns. I did eventually end up in Savannah. Prior to settling there, there were jaunts to London, Paris, Monte Carlo. Always the adventurer, always the wanderer, always searching. I began spending time in Tampa again and found that my old friends were still there and many of them had changed but most had not. I wish that I could say that I have changed or that I haven't slipped up now and again; but that is a work in progress. In the end we are who we are and we do what we have to do. Girls like me never have it easy. It's a hard, dark place to be sometimes but it's the life I chose for myself. Life in the fast lane has been tricky. It has left me empty and disappointed. It has left me alone. I have spent much of my life looking for love. I have found it but it's elusive. Men have never been a problem for me. But being desired is not the same as being loved. Happy at last? Not always...but working on it. What I have learned most of all was this-If the amazing ride I took is what it took to get me here- comfortable with myself, finally- I would do it all again. I would live the same, love the same, dream the same and make the same mistakes. If there is indeed a reason I should feel differently, I have yet to find it. Regret is pointless, a wasted emotion.

Wasn't it Dr. Seuss who said **"Be who you are and say what you feel, because those who mind don't matter, and those who matter don't mind."** I always found it funny, the logic that can sometimes come from children's books. The truth is, I have known happiness. I have loved and been loved by extraordinary men. I am where I want to be. *I AM WHO I WANT TO BE* and I had a blast getting here, despite everything. I **LIVED**...and I continue to live and love and dream and hope. And when all is said and done, isn't that what life is all about?

CHAPTER 70

Whatever became of...

I have been very fortunate to know many fascinating characters in my life, some not touched on in this book. Actors, rockers, politicians...As I previously stated, I have kept many stories to myself and changed the names whenever appropriate. Here is a list of what became of the people I knew. These provocative, compelling people who changed me in ways you cannot imagine. Over the years, I lost touch with many. Whenever possible, I have tried to track them down but many are "lost" to me. In the order they appeared...

Josette...
> Now a mother of two beautiful boys. It has been difficult for us to remain close. Sometimes the past has a way of doing that to people. But we will always remain bonded by the turmoil of our childhood and the long hard struggle to move past it. I love her, with all of my heart and though I don't speak with her everyday, she is never far from my thoughts and prayers.

My cousin Celeste...
> Still happy, still as open and loving as ever. Her beautiful daughter Rhiannon is grown now and pursuing a career in music.

Ruben/Lissette...
> Still, my best friend in the world. After Tampa, she moved to Vegas for five years. She is as beautiful as ever, inside and out. She continues to work as a danc-

er and a model. No longer the party girl, she gave up drugs long ago and remains clean and happy.

Esme. . .

Still beautiful, she continues to perform in Tampa.

Francisco. . .

After nearly ten years of not speaking, we finally saw each other again. He is still the same...funny, full of life. He always had faith in me. He still does. I wish him all the happiness in the world.

Ken. . .

My old roommate who provided temporary shelter for me at the beginning of my changes, is now in Central Florida. Happy and still with his boyfriend.

Ricky. . .

Ricky remains an always stellar presence in my life. The world of gay days and drag far behind him, he has reinvented himself as a makeup artist for a major label. He struggles daily to become a better person, a happier person. I have faith in him.

Hector. . .

After years of an on again off again friendship, we are finally on again. We have both grown. He remains a dear friend though his presence in my life is not as strong as it once was. I love him dearly. He is a good person. His wit and ability to laugh at others as well as himself is contagious. He is still Tampa's most in demand hairdresser and remains a club favorite to this day.

Hiran:. . .

Though I only briefly mentioned Hiran, it should not be an indicator of his importance to me. He is a genuine person with a kind, giving spirit. I love him so much. He continues to love me unconditionally to this day.

Liza...

I touched very little on Liza in my book but suffice to say she was an enormous influence in my life. She remains to this day one of the most dynamic individuals I've ever known. Her lust for life is second to none. She lives life her way, on her terms. She makes no excuses and doesn't give a damn what anyone thinks. In some ways, her and I are very much alike. She is a strong woman with weaknesses, like all of us.

Vidal...

Vidal is still in Key West and as colorful as happy as ever.

Connie...

After completing her sex change surgery, Connie got married and moved to Europe for several years. She now lives in America and is still happily married and still beautiful.

Sierra...

I still see and speak with Sierra. She is and will probably always be one of the great friends of my life. She is still the most beautiful woman I have ever laid eyes on.

Dominique/Tish...

Time has been hard to Tish but she takes it all in stride. She was recently diagnosed with cancer and is struggling to get better. Her quick wit intact, she was in high spirit's the last time we spoke. I will always wish her well.

Eric. . .

Last time I saw Eric, he was no longer the muscle man I remembered. But he was clean and happy and living in New York.

Jason. . .

He lives in South Beach with his boyfriend of several years and is as gorgeous as ever.

Keith. . .

My first shot at living with a man who wasn't more than a boy. Keith is now a man. He divides his time between New York and Boston and is the proud father of a beautiful baby girl.

Andrew. . .

My former lover is now living in South Florida. After being arrested for cocaine possession with intent to distribute, he went legit. He lives a quiet life far from the madness he was a part of. We no longer speak but I wish him well.

Anthony Lavelle. . .

I never saw Anthony again. I was told that he fled the country but really know nothing more about him or what happened to him.

"David". . .

I ran into David years after the Ft. Lauderdale incident in Boston. I was working for an "agent" one summer and he had responded to an ad hoping that it was me. I turned him away at the door. I never saw him again.

Bo. . .

Bo is still in Los Angeles. As far as I know, he no longer works in the porn industry.

Sebastian...

Sebastian now lives in New York City. I ran into an old friend from our south beach days at a club in NYC who says he currently works as a designer.

"Jessie"...

After a brief decline in his career, Jessie is back on top. His movies continue to do well...and I still smile whenever I hear him laugh.

Pasquale Devane...

Pasquale died in 2001, after a long struggle with AIDS. Xotica was never put into mass production. He had intended to publish and market the project himself to insure complete artistic control. Unfortunately, that never happened. Most of the photographs disappeared. But I will always remember my time in Greece. And what a special human being he was.

The Cast of Xotica...

The seven beautiful models I worked with in Greece are all but lost to me. I did run into Thalia on Ocean Drive in South Beach about two years ago. She was as beautiful as ever. And as mysterious. She offered no information as to what she had been up to. Only that she was living in Europe and that she had had a son.

Jillian...

My relationship with Jillian took an unusual turn. After several years of close friendship, we no longer see or speak to each other. Believe it or not it had nothing to do with the publication of this book which she always supported. The reasons will remain between us...suffice to say, she is not the woman I thought she was. But life goes on. It's full of surprises.

And I have learned that just about everyone has the capability to disappoint you. And most will.

Beth. . .

Beth is happy and clean. She too has moved on and continues to work as a hairdresser though she no longer dances or engages in the kind of craziness that marked that wild summer of love. She is a good mother and a kind friend.

Christine. . .

Christine remains my rock. Solid, non judgmental and honest. She has lived the hard life but she prevailed. She remains in a loving relationship with her girlfriend of six years and is pursuing a career in real estate. I consider her to be one of the most positive influences of my life and wish her nothing but the best.

Jim. . .

As far as I know, He is happy and living his dream. I will always love him and remember that time on The Key as the happiest time of my life. He is special in so many ways. I will never, ever forget him. For countless, beautiful reasons.

Made in the USA